CW01506517

The Internet of Animals

The Internet of Animals

Human–Animal Relationships in the Digital Age

Deborah Lupton

polity

Copyright © Deborah Lupton 2023

The right of Deborah Lupton to be identified as Author of this Work has been asserted in accordance with the UK Copyright, Designs and Patents Act 1988.

First published in 2023 by Polity Press

Polity Press
65 Bridge Street
Cambridge CB2 1UR, UK

Polity Press
111 River Street
Hoboken, NJ 07030, USA

All rights reserved. Except for the quotation of short passages for the purpose of criticism and review, no part of this publication may be reproduced, stored in a retrieval system or transmitted, in any form or by any means, electronic, mechanical, photocopying, recording or otherwise, without the prior permission of the publisher.

ISBN-13: 978-1-5095-5274-0
ISBN-13: 978-1-5095-5275-7 (pb)

A catalogue record for this book is available from the British Library.

Library of Congress Control Number: 2022944968

Typeset in 11 on 14 pt Sabon
by Cheshire Typesetting Ltd, Cuddington, Cheshire
Printed and bound in Great Britain by TJ Books Ltd, Padstow, Cornwall

The publisher has used its best endeavours to ensure that the URLs for external websites referred to in this book are correct and active at the time of going to press. However, the publisher has no responsibility for the websites and can make no guarantee that a site will remain live or that the content is or will remain appropriate.

Every effort has been made to trace all copyright holders, but if any have been overlooked the publisher will be pleased to include any necessary credits in any subsequent reprint or edition.

For further information on Polity, visit our website: politybooks.com

Contents

Acknowledgement

The writing of this book was partly funded by the Australian Research Council Centre of Excellence for Automated Decision-Making and Society (grant CE200100005).

Introduction

The Twitter and related Instagram accounts entitled 'Cats Being Weird Little Guys' feature images of cats in unusual positions or poses, or behaving in ways that most people would think of as human. There are cats standing at an oven, staring intently through the glass oven door at a pizza being baked within; cramming themselves inside unusual places such as the innards of a desktop computer, a refrigerator, a washing machine, a wastepaper basket or boot; riding on the backs of other animals, such as waterfowl; apparently using a computer, or a bank cash machine to withdraw money; dressed in human-style clothing; and displaying extreme facial expressions or contorted bodily positions.

Several dominant trends in representations of animals in popular culture can be discerned in these portrayals. First, there is the rendering of animals' bodies, habits and lives into digitized images shared globally on social media platforms. Second, the title of this social media account ('Cats Being Weird Little Guys') combines the name of the species that is often presented as dominating the internet (the domestic cat) with the words 'weird little guys'. The anthropomorphism of this phrase is

striking, as is the indication that it is about the humor-
ous or unusual ways in which cats behave. These images
are presented in ways that commodify and depersonalize the cats that are shown, rendering them as objects
for human entertainment. Third, these images encapsulate many of the tensions and contradictions pervading
contemporary ideas and responses to animals that can
be discerned across popular culture. Some of the images'
'weirdness' and accompanying entertainment value lies
in the ways that cats are shown as almost, but not quite,
human. Other images play on the very unhuman 'cat-
like' nature of these animals: cats' curiosity and their
capacities for agility, twisting their bodies into unusual
positions or squeezing into tight spaces. Cats are portrayed simultaneously as 'little guys' and 'weird', as
both 'cute' and 'amusing'. Finally, these digital feline
images and humans' responses to them online are suf-
fused with ambivalent emotional forces: enchantment
and amusement, but also hints of contempt and aggression, sometimes bordering on cruelty.

These powerful affects are central to how people
understand and feel about their relationships with cats
and other animals in contemporary societies, in which
close connections and emotional ties are routinely developed, online or with mobile devices, not only between
people but also as part of human–animal relationships.
At the same time as people are becoming increasingly
interested and emotionally invested in other animals,
digital technologies such as websites, social media platforms, apps, mobile or wearable devices, robotics and
automated decision-making technologies are playing
an ever more prominent role in their everyday lives
(Lupton, 2015, 2020b). Applying concepts and terms
from the natural world to new digital technologies is
a longstanding practice. We already routinely draw

on organic and ecological metaphors and images: the World Wide 'Web', computer 'viruses', 'cloud' computing, the 'rivers' or 'tsunamis' of big data, artificial 'intelligence (AI)', 'neural' networks, digital 'twins' . . . to name merely a few (Lupton, 2021). Such biophilic language conveys the deep affective and meaningful relationships humans have with nature, and the recognition that nature and culture are intertwined (Thomas, 2013). In turn, an expanding body of knowledge on how nonhuman living things communicate with each other through complex entanglements of underground rhizomatic fungal and tree root networks has led to metaphors referring to digital technologies, such as 'the Wood Wide Web', being used to describe relational connections between organic agents (Helgason et al., 1998).

Digital technologies are used to understand and document living entities and ecosystems in a rapidly expanding configuration of 'smart' devices, software and digital data. Just as a plethora of details about people's bodies, habits, practices and movements in space have become increasingly rendered into digital formats, thereby creating reams of digital data about them (Lupton, 2016, 2019b; Lupton et al., 2022), so, too, animals' bodies and lives are increasingly digitized and datafied. While it is often half-jokingly claimed that 'the internet is made of (or ruled by) cats', there are now many more animal species that are portrayed or monitored with the use of digital media and devices: including other companion animals, farm animals, animals in captivity and wild animals. These technologies promote the rapid generation and dissemination of images and information about animals across social networks, facilitate novel ways of monitoring animals' activities and geolocation, and use their appearance and behaviour to convey or modify human feeling.

The Internet of Animals

The Internet of Animals is the first book to bring
together perspectives from across the humanities and
social sciences to consider how digital technologies are
contributing to human–animal relationships at both the
micropolitical and macropolitical levels. It builds on and
extends a growing interest in social and cultural inquiry
in: (i) the digitization and datafication of humans and
other animals with and through new digital media and
'smart' devices; (ii) the affective and embodied relationships between humans and other animals; (iii) the health
and environmental crises in which human health and
wellbeing are inextricably entangled with those of other
animals and living creatures; and (iv) more-than-human
theoretical perspectives. The book delves into the ways
that animals across a range of species and in a multitude
of spaces are represented and incorporated into various
forms of digital technologies, and the consequences for
how we think and feel about, as well as relate to and
treat, other animals.

Across the book's chapters, the broader socioeconomic, cultural, biological and geographical contexts in
which these technological interventions have emerged
and are implemented are carefully considered. Many
animal species are becoming threatened by catastrophic
changes to their habitats and lives caused by humans,
such as ecological degradation and pollution; climate
change, global warming and extreme weather events;
and the clearing of forests to make way for industries or
the expansion of cities. Animals' health and wellbeing
have been severely undermined by these human-wrought
crises, including exacerbating their exposure to disease,
depriving them of their usual food sources, disrupting breeding cycles, accelerating species extinction and
contributing to biodiversity loss. Industries devoted
to the mass production of digital technologies (mobile

4

and other computing devices, WiFi, and digital data storage facilities) and to energy generation to power these technologies, together with the accumulation of non-degradable 'e-waste' from discarded devices and additional landfill toxins, make a massive contribution to these detrimental effects on planetary health. Digital media play a major role in drawing public attention to cases of animal mistreatment and cruelty, but also contribute to the objectification of animals and the vilification of species deemed to be threats to human welfare or the economy, requiring tight containment or extermination.

I write from the perspective of a privileged white person living in the Global North who has never had to suffer famine or food insecurity. I do not identify as an animal rights activist, but I support – and sometimes campaign for – environmental politics. I fear for and care about the health, welfare and futures of other humans and the other creatures that inhabit our planet (flora and fauna). These personal experiences and perspectives, together with my academic research expertise and interests, are the foundation of the arguments I advance in this book. I want to provoke thought by surfacing unsettling ideas, practices and feelings, and raising (but not necessarily answering) difficult questions about human–animal relationships in the digital age.

In choosing *The Internet of Animals* as the book's title, I have sought to encapsulate diverse modes of digitization and datafication of animals by playfully building on the established 'Internet of Things' (IoT) terminology. My conceptualization of the Internet of Animals encapsulates both the internet *of* animals and the internet *and* animals. The IoT is commonly used to describe 'smart' devices that are interconnected, exchanging digital data with each other. An oft-used definition is that put forward by the Organisation for Economic Co-operation and Development (OECD) (2016: 4): 'The IoT refers to an ecosystem in which applications and services are driven by data collected from devices that sense and interface with the physical world.' The IoT has been made possible by technological developments such as smaller and cheaper sensors, reliable ubiquitous wireless connections, mobile devices, improved software for managing large data sets, and an ecosystem for the generation, processing and storing of data, in conjunction with the emergence of the digital data economy (Maras and Wandt, 2019). To some extent, the Internet of Animals title, as I use it in this book, draws on the IoT, but it is also much broader and more inclusive. For my purposes, the Internet of Animals includes both these well-established technologies and novel and emerging devices and software of the type commonly referred to as 'smart' technologies. A huge variety of animals are imbricated in and with the latest digital technologies. These devices and media include mobile apps and wearable devices, memes and GIFs, drones, surveillance cameras, livestreaming services and robotic devices.

Concepts such as 'smart cities' and 'smart homes' make reference to the IoT. Animals inhabit these spaces and are therefore part of the IoT. Additionally, a vast array of 'smart' technologies has emerged to monitor, control and protect farm animals and wildlife and to support environmental sustainability, better farm productivity and the improved management of domesticated and wild animals. The phrase 'the Internet of Animals' has been used before, but with a much more specific focus, describing the ICARUS Global Monitoring with Animals initiative (ICARUS stands for International

Cooperation for Animal Research Using Space). One of the ICARUS website pages bears the heading 'The internet of animals' and goes on to describe how this organization is using digital sensor devices to track remotely the behaviour and movements of wildlife such as migratory birds and bats (ICARUS, 2022). The concept of the 'smart farm' similarly builds on the IoT to present visions of how animals and other living entities in agricultural settings can be digitized and datafied. Smart farming includes the deployment of devices such as sensors used to monitor soil, farm animals, water and plants. The big data generated by machines such as smart tractors, robotic harvesting technologies and environmental monitoring sensors are positioned as means to determine more accurately and precisely how to control such factors as moisture levels in soils, pests, fertilizer use and the movements of animals. Some smart agriculture initiatives are also addressing wider environmental issues such as climate change, land care, pollution and biodiversity (Klerkx et al., 2019).

In addition to the IoT, many other digital technologies are in place that capture and share images and other digital data about animals. Since the 1990s, the internet and World Wide Web have offered opportunities for providing and sharing information about animals and creating local and global social networks through the use of websites, online discussion forums and blogs. Computer games have frequently featured animal avatars. From the early 2000s, social media platforms such as Facebook, Instagram, Twitter, Tumblr, Snapchat and Reddit, messaging apps such as WhatsApp, Facebook Messenger, Weibo, Telegram and WeChat, and content-sharing sites, including YouTube, Pinterest and TikTok, have facilitated such interactions and relationships.

There is accumulating evidence, most often elicited in surveys conducted by companies or organizations in the pet or veterinary industry, that people are turning to online sources and apps to find and share information about their companion animals. Pet owners use the internet to seek advice about their pets and to order the best new products on offer for them (Animal Medicines Australia, 2019; Stojanovic, 2022a). A study of dog and cat owners who used Facebook found that approximately half of them reported using that platform's groups to give or receive pet advice from other members (Kogan et al., 2021). A 2017 industry survey of 2,000 American pet owners who used social media (cited in Aspling et al., 2018) found that 65% said that they posted about their pet on social media on average twice a week, and one in six had created a profile for their pet. One-third of the respondents said that they posted about their pets with around the same frequency as they uploaded content about their human family members. Of Australian pet owners surveyed in 2019 by Animal Medicines Australia (2019), 5% had installed home monitoring cameras for them, 7% had participated in pet-owner social media forums, and 5% had opened a social media account for their pets.

Throughout the book, I analyse the content and use of these devices, software and media from a sociocultural perspective, identifying implications for human–animal relationships and for generating ideas about future developments for digital technologies that have the potential to contribute to both human and nonhuman animal flourishing across the world. I argue that the ways in which animals are portrayed, monitored and cared for by humans using digital media and devices have significant implications for how humans and animals will live together in the near future: including human and animal health and wellbeing, environmental sustainability and activism, and industries related to digital technology development, animal care, animal protection, food production and consumption, smart homes and smart cities. I seek to contextualize digitized human–animal relationships within their more-than-digital contexts, acknowledging that digital technologies are always used in places and spaces in which other objects – both living and non-living – are present.

Contemporary human–animal relationships

There is an expanding literature devoted to examining the nature, meaning and moral dimensions of human–animal relationships, particularly in fields such as critical animal studies, the sociology of animals, ecofeminism, human–animal studies, animal ethics, critical post-humanities, environmental humanities, multispecies studies and animal geographies. While Western cultures in particular have sought to position humans as more-than-animal, and digital technologies are frequently used as part of this endeavour, a central premise of this book is that people are animals too, however much many of us like to forget or deny this reality. From this point onwards in the book, for simplicity's sake, when using the term 'animals' I will always mean 'nonhuman animals'.

In the contemporary era, a number of intersecting powerful affective and relational forces are combining to transform the ways that people are thinking, feeling and behaving in relation to other animals. These include the ever-expanding impulse towards anthropomorphizing animals; the rise and impact of cuteness cultures; the move towards positioning animals as therapeutic objects; growing interest globally in, and concern about, the health of the natural environment and the other living things that are part of ecosystems, including other animals; and a counter-discourse that represents animals/Nature as the dangerous Other. Digital technologies have contributed to the intensification of all these phenomena, all of which are at least partly responses to the socioeconomic and health crises that have erupted over the past few decades.

People are becoming much more sentimental about and attached to animals: particularly warm-blooded furry mammals and those they keep as companion animals (Fox and Gee, 2019). More than 67% of US households own at least one pet (Puac, 2022), with a similar proportion (61%) in Australia (Animal Medicines Australia, 2019) and (at 62%) in the UK (Statista, 2022). The UK figure is an increase of 15% in the past decade, with a large increase in 2020 and 2021 (Statista, 2022). A dominant trend in these affective connections is the anthropomorphizing of pets: particularly of dogs and cats. These companion animals are now treated by many people in the Global North as part of their families, close to bearing the status of children (as suggested by the commonly used terms 'fur babies' and 'pet parents'). Pet owners are also expected to take responsibility for caring for and controlling their companion animals far more than in the past (Fox and Gee, 2019).

A survey of Australian pet owners in 2019 found that most saw their dogs and cats as beloved family members. This status is reflected in the most popular names for these animals, many of which were common human names: Max, Bella, Charlie, Chloe, Lucy, Leo or Felix. Of these pet owners, 37% described themselves as a 'pet parent', 47% allowed their pet to sleep on the same bed, and 35% left on the heating/cooling, lights or television/

radio for their animals when the respondent was out of the home. The respondents described the joy of spending time with their pets, the unconditional love and companionship they felt they received from the animals, the feeling of having a purpose in their lives in caring for their pets, the positive impact on their health and mental wellbeing, and being unable to imagine life without their pets (Animal Medicines Australia, 2019). In the US, more than 50% of both dog and cat owners give their pets a gift at Christmas (Puac, 2022). Pet deaths are acknowledged and grieved more publicly than in previous eras, with owners typically representing the loss as equivalent to the death of a family member and often using social media to announce the death (Behler et al., 2020).

A large and rapidly developing industry has sprung up to respond to an increase in companion animal ownership. In the UK, this expenditure was estimated at close to £8 billion in 2020, up from almost £3 billion in 2005 (Statista, 2022). In the USA, pet expenditure was estimated at US$123 billion in 2021 and has been steadily growing year on year (Stojanovic, 2022b). Much of this spending, which was spurred by the conditions of the COVID-19 pandemic, goes on pet food, veterinary care, grooming, boarding services, pet clothing and health insurance (Puac, 2022; Stojanovic, 2022b). When once pets were euthanized with barely a thought if they developed a serious medical condition, their lives are now often extended by the kind of expensive surgery that humans have. They can have hip or knee replacement operations, surgery for cancer and are prescribed drugs to treat anxiety. Puppies attend 'puppy preschool' to be trained in compliant behaviour.

Animals are becoming drawn into human wellness cultures, used as therapy objects or to alleviate loneliness. This use of animals builds on a trend in recent decades for 'animal-assisted therapy', where 'therapy pets' (mostly dogs, but sometimes cats, rabbits or guinea pigs) are brought into healthcare settings as a way of helping people to develop communication skills and improve depression or anxiety, or to provide distraction and emotional comfort to ill people in those spaces (Krause-Parello et al., 2019). More broadly, as part of mainstream wellness cultures, animals are employed in workplaces and educational institutions as objects to alleviate stress and to provide companionship: for example, bringing baby animals to schools and universities to alleviate students' exam stress. As Claire Parkinson (2019: 97) observes: 'increasingly nonhuman animals are valued not for their "practical" use but for their emotional labour'. These affective attachments have only intensified during the COVID-19 crisis. The difficult conditions experienced by people around the world from the onset of the pandemic in early 2020, when many were faced with isolation, loneliness, mental distress and 'touch hunger' (Lupton, 2022), have led to a focus on achieving better health and wellbeing by interacting with animals: both online and face to face. Studies have demonstrated the comfort and solace that people gained from interacting with and feeling connected to animals, other living things and landscapes during the COVID crisis (Lupton and Lewis, 2022; Packer et al., 2021).

Cuteness cultures (referred to as *kawaii* culture, or *kawaisa* in Japanese) are a major driver of contemporary human–animal relationships: at least for a highly select group of species. In Japanese, *kawaii* means 'lovable', 'cute' or 'adorable' and refers to people or things that are pretty or dependent, including human and animal infants and older people (Nittono et al., 2021).

———

Introduction

In contemporary English, the word 'cute' is associated with sweetness, guilelessness and vulnerability (Nittono et al., 2021). While *kawaii* is culturally Japanese, it has found universal appeal outside Japan, contributing to both economic and cultural power for that nation (Allison, 2004; Kanesaka, 2022). Anthropologist Ann Allison (2004: 34–5) defines *kawaii* culture in English as involving attachments to imaginary creations or creatures with resonances both to childhood and to traditional Japanese culture. The history of cute aesthetics is usually traced back to the Edo period in Japan (1603–1868), but *kawaii* culture dramatically expanded in that country in the 1970s, then moving to East Asia and, more recently, Western cultures. *Kawaii* culture was positioned as offering the power of healing (initially in the post-World War II context in a devastated Japan) by generating feelings of tenderness and care, together with nostalgic appreciation of nature and tradition – essentially, a simpler, more intimate and less stressful world (Kanesaka, 2022).

The academic scholarship on cute affect was developed in the 1940s, led by German ethologist Konrad Lorenz, whose speciality was animal behaviour. He observed that infant humans and other animals tended to share similar physical features, which he called the 'baby schema': small bodies in relation to large round heads, large foreheads, short thick appendages, clumsy movements and large low-set eyes. Lorenz argued that these features evoked protective feelings in adults towards human infants, thereby acting as a survival mechanism that ensured that helpless babies would be nurtured (Dale et al., 2017). While most psychologists now dispute that such responses are instinctive rather than acculturated, or see them as a combination of both (Dale et al., 2017), the principles of appeal as outlined by Lorenz remain readily apparent in contemporary times in terms of which animals are deemed to be 'cute' and which are not. For example, a cross-cultural study involving participants in Japan, the US and Israel (Nittono et al., 2021) found that, while there were minor differences in how cuteness was defined, most features were universal across these nations. It is notable that infant animals were considered cuter than human infants in the participant group as a whole.

Cuteness as an affective force or aesthetic quality tends to be portrayed as trivial, facile, sentimental and feminized: not a 'serious' feeling or value, despite abundant evidence of how capacious this feeling is and the diverse effects it has on people's use of the internet and social media, together with its economic value in commodity culture (Dale et al., 2017; Meese, 2014). Animals deemed to be cute receive a huge amount of attention on the internet – particularly in social and visual media. In what has been described as the internet 'cute economy' coming together with the participatory culture fostered by social media and online discussion forums (Meese, 2014), users of the internet have profited in creating and sharing appealing images of animals. The 'Grumpy Cat' internet meme is perhaps the most well known of the many animal-related images featuring amusing or cute animals that have circulated for some years. However, Grumpy Cat is only one of countless cat memes, GIFs and videos available online, along with many other portrayals of animals that are considered appealing.

A greater sensitivity and concern towards the welfare and wellbeing of the natural environment and ecological systems are also contributing to shifts in people's feelings about other animals. Images of animals are used by activist organizations to provoke strong affective responses as part of initiatives to fight animal cruelty.

Among wild animals, the koala, even as an adult animal, fits Lorenz' schema perfectly, with its large round head, low set eyes, stocky body, short appendages and waddling gait. Koalas are often to be found in 'cute animal' digital portrayals and are strategically used as charismatic flagship species in conservation awareness and fundraising efforts (Bergman et al., 2022). While cute affects play some role in these affective connections, broader ethical principles concerning animal rights and the awe-inspiring power and beauty of nature are central to these transformations. A notable move towards attunement to issues such as animal welfare in farming, the horse and greyhound racing industries and the fur industry, together with heightened awareness of the environmental impacts of factory farming, is evident in the wealthy countries comprising the Global North. Many people have adopted an ethical stance on the treatment and use of animals and are changing their consumption habits accordingly. Practices such as the adoption of organic, vegetarian and vegan diets are also expanding rapidly in response to concern about animal welfare and environmental sustainability (Kalte, 2021).

On the other hand, however, millions of animals, including both domesticated and wild animals, are still widely exploited for the benefit of humans: bred or captured to provide food, clothing, medicinal therapies or companionship. Some animals have become increasingly vilified and subject to containment and control, including 'pest' species such as bed bugs, mice and insects that eat crops (Feber et al., 2017; Taylor and Twine, 2014). Furthermore, animals have become increasingly portrayed by the news media as dangerous in health risk discourses. Such crises as 'mad cow' disease, dioxin in chickens, salmonella in eggs and transspecies viral infections that have caused pandemics such as the avian and swine influenza, together with news media reports of wild or domesticated animals that have attacked humans, have positioned animals as the source of illness, injury, infection and death. Media coverage of these animal-related risks has raised the spectre of savage, diseased or mutated species created by humans' meddling into 'natural' processes (Molloy, 2011).

An intriguing feature of digital media portrayals of the COVID-19 crisis involved visual images and narratives shared on social media sites that purported to demonstrate the renewed habitation of urban spaces by domestic or wild animals (goats in the streets of a Welsh town, dolphins in the Venetian canals, kangaroos leaping down city byways in the Australian cities, wild boars gathering close to major roads in Barcelona). Some of the images were fake, or from pre-COVID times. Nonetheless, they drew attention to the role of humans in the emergence of the new coronavirus SARS-CoV-2. So, too, reporting of wet markets in the city of Wuhan, China, where the first COVID cases were identified, emphasized humans' mistreatment of wild animals as part of the wildlife trade, and their incursion into animals' habitats. Questions were raised in these media concerning whether the pandemic was 'nature striking back' at humans for their abuse and mindless exploitation of animals and other living things (Lupton, 2022).

These types of portrayals reflect the ambivalence felt by humans towards nature. Nature is positioned in some representations as the superior, pure Other to the Self of humanity, but in others as contaminated, wild, out of control and highly dangerous to human health and wellbeing. These dangerous animals are positioned in some cases as liminal – such as domesticated dogs that seem almost human-like but which then may turn on humans and attack them; and hybrid – such as 'mad cows' that have consumed other animals' remains and thus been transformed by human action from herbivores to carnivores, or trans-species viruses that are able to cross between humans and other animal species. In recent times, wild animals such as bats, civets and pangolins have been linked to serious outbreaks of infectious diseases in humans, such as the SARS and COVID-19 pandemics, which involved transmission of viruses from wild animals that had been captured for human consumption. For example, millions of farmed mink in Denmark were slaughtered due to the concern that they harboured and spread the coronavirus causing COVID-19 (Murray, 2020). Such culls demonstrate the positioning of animals as economic commodities, rather than living beings worthy of protection, with animal disease portrayed as a trade issue rather than an animal health and wellbeing concern (Coghlan et al., 2021; Riley, 2022).

Animal–human–digital assemblages

Perspectives that social researchers have used previously to understand the implications of the ways that humans are digitized and datafied, and the affective connections established between people with and through digital media and devices, can be brought to bear to understand how these technologies are employed to portray and monitor other animals. In so doing, we can ask fundamental questions not only about people's experiences of digital societies and cultures, but also about how concepts of 'the human' and 'the animal' are defined and the human–animal relationship is understood and performatively practised.

Research on the use of digital platforms such as online discussion forums and social media has demonstrated the value of such media for making and reinforcing relational and affective connections with others. In what have been described as 'the sharing economy' (John, 2017) and the generation of 'networked intimacy' and 'digital intimate publics' (Dobson et al., 2018), these platforms can configure strong affective ties between people who may never have met in person or even know each other's real names. The sharing economy relies on users of such platforms to share all kinds of information about themselves or about their interests and passions. Users of these sites can find an intense sense of community and intimacy with other users, centred around shared interests or concerns such as health problems, fandom and life stage. Other users are invited to respond by making comments; providing feedback or advice; using 'like', emojis and other symbols demonstrating affective responses; or by sharing the content with other internet or app users. Visual media such as selfies, GIFs, memes and YouTube or TikTok videos are ways of visually encapsulating feelings and opinions, and therefore offer opportunities for people to convey these feelings readily to others online. These images generate the most resonance and power (and 'become viral') when they provoke or inspire strong affective forces.

Despite the proliferation of digital technologies and their major implications for human–animal relationships, human and animal health and wellbeing, and the economy, surprisingly little research in the humanities and social sciences has been conducted into these phenomena. Several volumes have been published over the past decade or so that have explored how animals are portrayed in popular culture, but they have mostly focused on legacy media rather than contemporary digital media. For instance, *Popular Media and Animals* by

Claire Molloy (2011) covers newspaper reporting and television and film portrayals, with some analyses of how animal activism, hunting, laboratory animals, farm animals, wildlife, celebrity animals and monstrous animals are portrayed in these media. Randy Malamud's *An Introduction to Animals and Visual Culture* (2012) focuses on media such as artworks, photographs, pornography, advertisements, children's books and film, tracing the history of visual representations of animals back to Ice Age cave paintings. He makes a key point in the book that many people in the Global North living in urban environments are more likely to encounter animals via the mass media than living creatures in the course of an average day (with the important exception of pets).

The edited volume *Critical Animal and Media Studies* (Almiron et al., 2015) brings together critical media studies with critical animal studies, with a strong animal advocacy orientation. Chapters explore the portrayal of animals in the news media, television programmes, film and other popular media, but there is little reference to digital cultures. Brett Mills' *Animals on Television: The Cultural Making of the Non-Human* (2017) identifies the sheer volume of portrayals of animals in contemporary television – including documentaries about wild or farm animals or veterinary practitioners, animated anthropomorphic animals in children's programmes, and cooking shows (as meat included in recipes). One of the most well-known introductory books on human–animal studies, *Animals and Society* by Margo DeMello (2021), was recently released in its second edition. There are three chapters in this expansive volume devoted to past and present cultural portrayals of animals (in symbol and art, religion and folklore, and literature and film) but none specifically about digital media.

In new media and internet studies, there is some recent evidence of interest in the use of digital media and devices to portray or monitor animals. Thus far, this literature focuses mostly on visual media such as YouTube videos, computer games and social media platforms such as Instagram, or on 'smart' technologies used for generating and processing digitized information about animals. A group of researchers in animal geographies scholarship has also devoted some attention to investigating the use of digital technologies for monitoring and datafying animals. A small sub-section of computer science research entitled 'animal–computer interaction studies' involves research into some aspects of digitized animals from a technology design perspective, including addressing technical and ethical issues. Legal studies and information ethics scholars have attempted to identify and evaluate how emerging technologies such as AI, machine learning and robotics can harm animals, with an eye to developing appropriate policy and regulation.

In this book, I draw on and synthesize this existing scholarship and extend it by adopting an overarching more-than-human theoretical argument. I position digital media and devices as vibrant agents in the animal–human–digital assemblages that form when humans and nonhuman animals gather. These are new and constantly changing assemblages that problematize how we understand the concepts of 'the human' and 'the animal'. A red thread in my analysis is an approach to agency that understands it as relational: distributed between and emergent from these lively gatherings of humans with digital media and other animals. Throughout the book's discussions, a series of questions are addressed, as follows: How are human–animal relationships changing, and how are digital media and devices contributing to this change? What do humans and other animals lose and gain when animals are digitized and datafied? What are the implications of a more-than-human approach to ethical and caring relationships between humans and other animal species? What are the implications for both human and animal health and wellbeing – and, at a larger scale, for planetary health?

In addressing these questions, I engage with the expanding body of more-than-human theory that focuses on the embodied and multisensory dimensions of people's encounters with digital technologies and digital data, and the affective forces and capacities that are generated with and through these relationships. My approach to digitization and datafication recognizes that digital technologies and digital data are vibrant agents in the lives of humans and animals, configuring animal–human–digital assemblages that are constantly changing as technologies come together with humans and animals in place, space and time. I bring together my longstanding interest in how people's bodies and identities are enacted and experienced with and through digital media and digital data (for example, Lupton, 1995, 2015, 2016, 2019b, 2020b; Lupton and Williamson, 2017; Lupton et al., 2022), digital health (Hjorth and Lupton, 2021; Lupton, 2017, 2019a, 2019c) and digital food cultures (Lupton, 2018, 2019d, 2020a), with a newer focus on the more-than-human dimensions of bioethics, planetary health and mutual flourishing (Lupton, 2020c, 2021, 2022). Throughout the book's chapters, I build on these perspectives to consider how people position themselves within more-than-human and more-than-digital worlds in these times of rapid social change and environmental and health crises.

Structure of the book

This book tackles an enormous scope, including a diverse and expansive array of technologies – far more than can be discussed in detail within its pages. Rather than attempt a wholly comprehensive examination of all the major modes of digitization and datafication of animals, the book describes and analyses several key examples, structured around topical themes. Relevant social and cultural theoretical perspectives are applied to identify the broader contexts and multispecies worlds in which digital devices and software have been imagined, designed and inserted into the everyday lives of humans and animals.

As part of my analysis, I identify the sociotechnical imaginaries used to define digital technologies used in relation to animals, and the meanings and promises they offer, and pay attention to the embodied practices, moral and ethical issues and affective forces that are part of these animal–human–digital assemblages. The concept of sociotechnical imaginaries relates to frameworks of culturally shared values and identities, forms of power–knowledge that draw from and shape people's responses to things like novel, emerging and future digital technologies. Imaginaries come together as part of sociomaterial assemblages of people, things and places when new technologies are made sense of and engaged with. They are configured by publics, government, industry, activists and other stakeholders across a range of media – from policy reports to social media platforms (Jasanoff, 2015).

Sociotechnical imaginaries are important to consider as they operate to frame novel technologies and invite engagement with them. Social researchers have demonstrated that discourses on novel digital technologies in industry, developer and government discussions frequently present techno-utopian imaginaries, in which these technologies are portrayed as offering innovative solutions and ways to optimize the economy, industrial production and transport systems, and improve citizens' everyday lives. They also generate useful data that can be employed for commercial, developmental or policy purposes (Lupton, 2015, 2019b, 2020a). Objects in the 'smart' technology universe are characterized in anthropomorphic terms as 'intelligent', 'sociable' and 'communicative' – in some cases, possessing capabilities beyond those of human intelligence and interactions. As is evident from other promotional representations of novel digital technologies such as AI and big data (Elish and boyd, 2018; Lupton, 2019b), a heightened sense of optimism is frequently put forward in these discussions. IoT technologies are often portrayed as almost magical in their capabilities and their power to be 'disruptive' and 'revolutionary' (Strengers et al., 2019b).

So, too, the affordances that are designed into digital technologies and promoted as part of the promissory narratives of technology developers are crucial elements of animal–human–digital assemblages. Like imaginaries, these material design features work to encourage people and other animals to interact with technologies in specific ways, based on how designers, developers, promoters and potential users of these technologies imagine or hope that they will be incorporated into people's lives (Nagy and Neff, 2015). As they come together with human and animal embodied capabilities and sensory knowledges, sociotechnical imaginaries and technological affordances can either open or close down capacities for action or agency (Lupton, 2019b). Throughout this book, I identify these technological imaginaries and affordances, referring to examples where novel digital technologies have been put to work in contexts involving animals. In so doing, I question the implications of these imaginaries, affordances and deployments for how we think, feel and relate to other animals, and reflect on the impacts for animals of our attempts to digitize and datafy them.

In early 2021, I conducted a short online survey with closed- and open-ended questions asking people about their use of digital media and devices in relation to animals – not only pets but any type of animal (the Appendix provides further details of the 'Animals on the Internet' project). While this survey is by no means representative, it provided some interesting insights into an under-researched topic. All the 130 participants responded 'yes' to the question: 'Have you ever used the internet to find information about your pet/s or any other animals?' Nearly all of these participants (97 per cent), most of whom lived with companion animals (85 per cent), reported uploading or sharing information about their pets or any other animals online. More detailed findings from the participants' responses to the open-ended questions are provided later in several of the book's chapters.

Chapter 1 introduces the foundational concepts and theoretical perspectives on human–animal relations offered from relevant scholarship across the humanities and social sciences, and discusses how they contribute to the key issues and themes discussed in the book. The next four chapters focus on specific ways in which animals are portrayed in digital media and monitored with the use of 'smart' technologies. Chapter 2 addresses the topic of animal activism and other political issues concerning humans' treatment of and relationships with animals, including contestation and conflicts between actors in this online space. In chapter 3, the plethora of rationales, imaginaries and practices configuring the dataveillance of animals are examined: including those devices designed for caring for pets or protection of wildlife, together with technologies incorporated into 'smart farming' initiatives. Chapter 4 focuses on the affective dimensions of cuteness and celebrity as they are expressed in relation to animals in digital media, and the positioning of animals as therapeutic objects. The representation of animals in computer games and zoomorphic robots are the subjects of chapter 5. While these digital technologies may seem quite distinct from each other, the strong influence of Japanese culture is evident in both modes for digitizing animals. The brief conclusion chapter summarizes the main points made in the book and provokes thinking about the futures of the Internet of Animals, with a particular focus on the use of digital technologies in arts-based initiatives that seek to attune humans to their role as merely one animal species in complex multispecies ecosystems.

I

Conceptualizing Humans, Animals and Human–Animal Relations

This chapter presents an overview of the theoretical perspectives and concepts that underpin the analysis of human–animal relations that is undertaken throughout the book. This discussion provides a springboard for surfacing and understanding the rationales, social imaginaries and practices that contribute to animal–human–digital assemblages. Changes in Western perspectives on humans and animals are traced from pre-modern to contemporary times, and the insights offered by more-than-human philosophies, including that of non-Western and First Nations' worldviews, are explained. The position of moral philosophy and animal ethics in considering the status of animals is contrasted with a more-than-human approach to recognizing the complexities of onto-ethico-epistemological dimensions of multispecies relations.

Humans and animals: Western conceptual approaches

Especially in the contemporary cultures of the wealthy countries constituting the Global North (which includes

Western countries located outside the northern hemisphere such as Australia and New Zealand), denial of the animal nature of humans is a frequent trope. Drawing on Christian belief and Cartesian divisions between mind and body, since the Enlightenment and the scientific revolution, philosophical and scientific perspectives on living creatures have increasingly sought to distinguish humans as both separate from, and superior to, other living things – including other animals (Chan, 2018; Chiew, 2014; TallBear, 2015). According to this dualistic conceptual opposition, the nonhuman animal is associated with dumb flesh, while the human (positioned as non-animal) is defined by rational thought (Chan, 2018). Simultaneously with worldviews which position people as separate from animals, there has emerged in Western cultures in the post-Enlightenment period a growing sentimentality about some (but not all) animals. This perspective does not necessarily grant equality of status to the animals at which it is directed, but it does position animals as more human-like than in recent eras, even if humans are not equally positioned as more animal-like.

The notion of Otherness pervades contemporary Western portrayals and treatment of both animals and humans, often based on concepts of control over the boundaries of the body. The ideal human body is tight, contained, exercising full control over what comes inside and goes outside. At its most extreme, this ideal disavows the very existence of the material body, seeking the perfection and purity of rational thought over the impurities of fleshly desires, affects and needs (Ahmed, 2004; Grosz, 1994; Shildrick, 1997). As cultural anthropologist Mary Douglas (Douglas, 1966, 1992) argued, that which is seen to be anomalous, difficult to classify, creates feelings of unease and repulsion. Otherness is a product of observations of difference/strangeness. Otherness is dangerous because it confounds order and control. The Other represents the unknown and the threat of loss of one's own identity through contact with this unknown, the dissipation of boundaries and the realization of our own limits. Otherness does not only involve that which is placed directly in opposition to the self/us, as part of a binary opposition, but also that which is uncertain, confusing and blurs the ordering of binary oppositions – the hybrid and the liminal. The liminal is that which represents a transitional, middle stage between two distinctly different entities, identities or sites. It thus cannot be categorized into either: it is 'in-between' (Kristeva, 1982).

The white, able-bodied, bourgeois, heterosexual and cisgendered masculine body is valued as most closely conforming to this idea of the contained, 'civilized' body. The bodies of women, members of the poor or the working class, people of colour, disabled people and queer or nonbinary people are frequently represented as Other – incapable of fully achieving this ideal. Such bodies are culturally represented as subject to the will of the flesh rather than that of reason, prone to emotionality, excessive desire, violence or disarray (Baquero et al., 2021; Belcourt, 2015; Plumwood, 2002). Bodies that are seen to transgress or blur culturally important boundaries are the source of confusion, fear, anxiety and even hatred, revulsion and disgust. Those things that are not easily categorized, that fail to stay in their categories, or that simply are too different from the self, tend to arouse anxieties and fears. They are culturally designated as potentially polluting and contaminating to the self. As a result, people or things that are categorized as Other are typically dealt with using exclusionary tactics that seek to locate them as far as possible, both symbolically and literally, from the self (Ahmed, 2004; Grosz, 1994; Shildrick, 1997).

The contemporary Western ideal of the individuated human body/self is only a few centuries old, emerging from social and political changes in the sixteenth century in Europe (Hartnell, 2018; Taylor, 1989). German sociologist Norbert Elias (1978) traced an increasing individuation of people's bodies/selves from each other, and a strengthening of awareness of human rights and initiatives against cruelty, violence, slavery and physical punishment, in his scholarship on 'the civilizing process' during the early modern period in Europe. Historical accounts have demonstrated that pre-modern Western concepts of human bodies/selves saw them as highly porous, entangled with each other and open to the more-than-human world. Everyday bodily functions often took place in public spaces, with little sense of shame or concerns about privacy, and public displays of violence and excessive indulgence were accepted. People and livestock often lived in the same spaces, and even strangers commonly shared beds or bedchambers when finding a place to sleep (Elias, 1978; Hartnell, 2018).

Legends and folklore circulating during the pre-modern era often depicted animals as taking on human form, or shapeshifting, becoming part of families by marrying humans and giving birth to children. Such narratives demonstrate a fluidity of boundaries between the human body/self and that of other animals. They positioned people as part of the natural world, as well as portraying strong ties of intimacy and kinship between humans and other animals and the importance of respecting the autonomy and agencies of animals (Blackie, 2021). Extreme cruelty to animals, however, was culturally accepted. Just as public beheadings and floggings of humans were common entertainments in pre-modern times, so too were displays of animal torture or killings, such as cockfights, bear or dog fights and rituals such as the mass burning of cats, simply for the pleasure of seeing them suffer (Elias, 1978).

Elias (1978) argued that, from the sixteenth century, wealthy Europeans began to move away from these beliefs and practices. Moderation became a virtue. There was a far greater focus on the regulation of emotions, the restraint of impulses, and the mastery of the body, as demonstrated by a growing set of rules about table manners, clean clothing and the appropriate ways and places to engage in sexual activity or expelling body wastes. Violent actions and cruelty towards other people became viewed as more repugnant. To some extent, these new values were extended towards animals. The torturing and killing of animals no longer took place as public spectacles, and slaughtering of animals for food was moved to sites that were less open to public view. However, ideas of 'civilized' behaviour were based on the notion that humans should not behave like animals: thus emphasizing the difference between humans as ideally rational, highly self-disciplined beings, and animals as irrational creatures ruled by their bodily impulses.

In the contemporary era, humans continue to be portrayed in Western thought as superior to and masters of all other living things by virtue of their capacity for reason and self-discipline over their bodies (Plumwood, 2002; Taylor and Twine, 2014; Tester, 1991). Despite some evidence of greater recognition of the needs and feelings of other animals, humans in most societies still treat them as Other to the self. The notion of human exceptionalism and superiority to all other species is used to support extractive, exploitative and often downright damaging and cruel practices directed at other members of the animal kingdom. Animals – even the most loved companion animals – are still treated as commodities and the property of humans, to be bought and sold at will. In current processes of industrialization and commodity capitalism, the economic value of animals for human benefit predominates in most regulations about their treatment. Farm animals and their products (offspring, flesh, milk, wool, eggs, feathers, skins) are managed as if they are industrial goods. Animals that are considered pests, disease carrying, not physically appealing or that are destined for the tables of humans continue to be killed or tortured – often with very little regard for the quality of their lives, their wellbeing, any pain and suffering they may endure, or the nature of their deaths (Mather, 2019; Riley, 2022). These practices have contributed to large-scale environmental devastation, species extinction and biodiversity loss across the planet, harming the health and wellbeing of all living things: human and nonhuman.

Social researchers are beginning to explore the social, cultural and political dimensions of animal life. An analysis of sociological writings on animals identified steadily growing interest in that discipline from the late 1970s, with a notable increase in interest from the early 2000s, accompanied by the introduction of specialist groups and streams in sociological associations (Taylor and Sutton, 2018). Sociologist Keith Tester's book *Animals and Society: The Humanity of Animal Rights* (1991), published over two decades ago, is a thoughtful exposition of the ambiguities in humans' relationships and thinking about animals. In the first lines of the book, Tester (1991: 1) argues that animals 'disgust and please us; we can do with them what we will yet pull back with horror from open cruelty'. While animal sociologies have tended not to be overtly politically oriented (Taylor and Sutton, 2018), contributors to the interdisciplinary field of critical animal studies devote attention to the social structural and ethical dimensions of humans' domination of and cruelty towards animals, including their domestication, breeding, husbandry, capture and slaughter by humans (Cudworth, 2015; McCance, 2012; Taylor and Twine, 2014).

Some critiques of people's treatment of animals have adopted Marxist-inspired political economy perspectives which focus on the economic dimensions of animals' exploitation (Taylor and Sutton, 2018). Feminist critiques, of which Carol Adams' book *The Sexual Politics of Meat* (1990) is one of the most well known, have sought to draw parallels between the ways that animals and women are mistreated and objectified in patriarchal societies. In a more recent analysis, Erika Cudworth (2015) argues for the inclusion of animals into sociological research agendas and priorities that focus on the sociology of violence. She writes about the manifold ways in which animals are subjected to various forms of violence, including hunting wild animals and fishing, and the mass killing of animals for food, and how these acts of violence are institutionalized and taken for granted across the globe. People do not usually view themselves as cruel predators: those who engage in or condone animal killing view such acts in economic terms or in relation to recreation or food needs, positioning animals solely as commodities. Cudworth shows that the scale of factory farming and animal killing, largely for human consumption, is historically unprecedented and is continuing to grow in scale.

Here again, parallels can be drawn between how humans who are considered 'like animals' and animals themselves are treated by members of 'civilized' social groups in positions of power and influence. Violence against animals has much in common with violence against humans who have been positioned in Western ontologies as 'less-than-human', including people of colour and First Nations people who were enslaved and colonized by settlers (TallBear, 2015). For example, persistent racialization has led to what Achilles Mbembe (2019) refers to as 'necropolitics', in which people of colour are considered expendable by powerful white groups and governments. Indeed, it has been argued that the oppression of both animals and colonized First Nations populations by the settler-colonialist state are parallel logics, propelled by a white supremacist viewpoint that positions both people of colour and animals as less worthy of life or agency. From this perspective, domesticated and wild animals and colonized subjects have been objectified, confined, killed and exploited in similar ways, based on settler-colonialist mentalities and practices of domination and control over those living beings that are deemed to be less than human (Belcourt, 2015).

Animal rights and moral philosophy

The issue of animal rights has long exercised philosophical debates. However, it is only in very recent times that animal rights initiatives have emerged, and these endeavours are confined to very specific contexts: mostly in high-income countries, among privileged social groups. Until the end of the eighteenth century, Enlightenment ideals that privileged human rationality and moral reasoning capacity meant that religious thought continued to insist that animals should not be an appropriate topic for the moral concern of humans, due to their ontological position as less than human, lacking the intelligence and reasoning capacities of humans. It was not until the issue was reframed as that of sentience – the ability to sense and understand experiences of the world, including to suffer and feel pain – that the passage of legislation against some forms of animal cruelty eventuated. It was decided that, even if animals lack the cognitive abilities of humans, the capacity for sentience that humans decided some species possessed was reason enough for them to be treated with compassion (Riley, 2022).

The field of animal ethics in the discipline of philosophy focuses directly on the moral dimensions of humans' relationships with other animals. This scholarship highlights the human-centric position that most people and social institutions, such as government and the legal system, adopt towards other animals. As Tester (1991) points out, the very terms 'animal rights' or 'animal liberation' in themselves plant a stake in the ground. They are claiming that animals should be bestowed with rights, or freedom from interference and cruelty. These terms represent a new focus on the wellbeing and welfare of animals. While philosophers have been pondering the moral dimensions of human–animal relationships since ancient times, scholarship in animal ethics as a subdiscipline of moral philosophy and a field of bioethics has grown rapidly over the past half-century, demonstrating greater interest, in societies in general, in animal welfare and rights (Kagan, 2018).

In this literature, animals are depicted as possessing intrinsic value, dignity and rights: creatures of worth with their own interior life, existing beyond the needs or desires of humans and deserving of our respect. 'Moral anthropocentrism' is rejected in the animal ethics scholarship – that is, the assumption that human needs, wants or desires should receive priority over those of animals. Animal ethicists challenge an instrumental approach to animals, in which they are treated as things or tools for the use of humans (Linzey and Linzey,

2018). Much of the mainstream animal ethics literature is devoted to considering the morality of acts such as factory farming, hunting, the trade in wildlife, the use of animals for research purposes and the slaughtering of animals for human use. Ethical appraisals also frequently include evaluation of legalistic rights and how these can be applied to animals as they are already to humans.

Australian moral philosopher Peter Singer's book *Animal Liberation* (1975), which he describes as discussing 'the tyranny of human over nonhuman animals' (Singer, 1975: ix) is one of the key texts in animal ethics and moral philosophy scholarship, as well as in animal activism. Singer's argument in this influential volume leans on the rationalist moral philosophical principle of utilitarianism. Utilitarianism traditionally weighs the morality of an individual's actions according to whether they promote pleasure or cause pain to other humans. Singer adopted this approach and applied it to animals, asking how people's actions contribute to animals' wellbeing or suffering. As Singer (1975) has argued, many people and social institutions adopt a 'speciesist' approach, in which members of the human species (*Homo sapiens*) are privileged over other animal species as bearing greater moral status because of their superior cognitive capacities. Singer strongly criticizes what he sees as the immoral pain, misery and suffering inflicted on animals simply because people see them as lesser species. He defines speciesism as similar to other forms of discrimination, prejudice and exclusion exercised by humans, such as racism and sexism. Singer argues that all animals should be 'treated as the independent sentient beings that they are', with the moral standards that are applied to humans equally applied to other animals (Singer, 1975: x). This approach is described by Singer as 'the principle of equal consideration of interests'. As he argues, this approach is not about being an 'animal lover' or sentimentally finding animals cute and cuddly, but rather applying rigorous moral philosophy thinking. Singer is a strong proponent of adopting vegetarian or vegan diets as a way of easily avoiding speciesism and the infliction of animal suffering.

Singer's writings are still dominant in animal rights activism and critical animal studies, which often demonstrate how the economic exploitation of people in industries such as factory farming, and places such as slaughterhouses, accompanies the mistreatment of animals in these locations. For such critics, concepts of solidarity must 'cross the species barrier' (Taylor and Taylor, 2020: 105). It is notable, however, that this Western move towards a perspective that recognizes both the rights of animals and their individuation from humans is an extremely selective position (Feber et al., 2017; Mather, 2019). Not all animals are equally treated in animal ethics or critical animal studies appraisals. The word 'animals' encompasses many different life forms and species: including not only other mammals but also invertebrates, reptiles, fish, birds and amphibians. Yet much of the discourse on animal rights and liberation is very specific, relating to animals that are most like humans (other mammals or vertebrates) and that serve some kind of purpose to humans. There tends to be far less concern about the wellbeing or protection of less appealing creatures such as snakes, slugs, snails, spiders, cockroaches, ants or mosquitoes, and parasitic animals such as hookworms, ticks, fleas or lice. These species remain positioned as the dangerous Other.

The concept of sentience is paramount in most analyses conducted by moral philosophers, legal scholars and scientists, who engage in debates about which animal species should be considered sufficiently sentient to be accorded rights (Mather, 2019). There is detailed discussion concerning to what extent various kinds of animals can be considered 'sentient' or have emotional responses, or how intelligent they are (that is, how much like humans they are), or to what degree they possess 'moral standing', and the implications of assessments of these attributes for the moral obligations people should exert in relation to other animals. In this approach to moral reasoning, animal species are placed on a continuum or hierarchy depending on how sentient and intelligent they are and how aware they are of their conditions of suffering and pain (Hagendorff et al., 2022; Kagan, 2018; Linzey and Linzey, 2018).

Philosophical inquiries into the ontologies, epistemologies and ethics of human–animal and human–digital relations become entangled when considering animal–human–digital assemblages. Discussions of the ways that digital technologies configure human–animal relationships or may harm animals, within orthodox legal and moral philosophy scholarship, have thus far been limited. When such analyses have been conducted, they tend to adopt a similar approach to that evident in the animal ethics literature. For example, Leonie Bossert and Thilo Hagendorff (2021) draw attention to the common comparisons made by AI researchers between animal cognition or sentience and machine learning, using animals as a benchmark in what they consider to be a demeaning way. They give the example of the 'Animal-AI-Olympics' competition among AI researchers, where they try to determine how close software has edged towards achieving the cognitive abilities of some animals. Bossert and Hagendorff view such comparisons as reproducing problematic assumptions about the limitations and deficiencies of animal intelligence compared with that of humans, or indeed of software. Such portrayals and uses of animals in AI research, they argue, reduce animals to cogs in machines or to digital data for experimental purposes, obviating any consideration of their welfare or individuality as sentient living creatures.

It is notable that Peter Singer has recently collaborated with scholars from the disciplines of computer science and information technology policy in a paper exploring what they term 'speciesist bias in AI' (Hagendorff et al., 2022). It is argued by these researchers that little attention has been paid to bias in AI towards animals, despite sustained analysis of unfair algorithms and digital data processing as it affects groups dealing with discrimination, such as women and people of colour. Hagendorff and colleagues see moral evaluations of the impact of AI technologies on animals as a logical extension of recent analyses in AI ethics in relation to humans. They assert that if the digital data sets on which AI applications such as machine learning and automated decision-making are trained are speciesist, this results in 'speciesist bias' in these applications, such as recommender and image recognition systems. They argue that the corollary of this bias is that violence against animals is normalized and perpetuated, rather than challenged. Thus, for example, Hagendorff and colleagues find it problematic that image recognition software uses terms such as 'hog', 'milk cow' and 'animals', and for dogs, 'hunting dog', 'working dogs', 'toy dogs' and so on. These terms are considered to be speciesist because they are defining these animals in terms of their economic or other use value to humans.

More-than-human perspectives

There is now a gradual, but increasingly prominent, turn towards acknowledging what non-Western epistemologies and concepts can offer to Western philosophy. As Giovanni Aloi (2022: 8) put it, in a recent editorial for a special issue of the cultural studies journal *Antennae* on 'beyond posthumanism®™' (*sic*), questions of 'Who is the human of posthumanism, who is the *anthropos* of the Anthropocene, and where does the animal of human–animal studies begin or end?' should be asked of the traditional posthuman approach. Western philosophy has been trenchantly criticized for the limitations of its humanistic foci. Not only has this body of thought privileged humans, scholars contributing to it have adopted an overwhelmingly male, white/European and colonialist focus, failing to engage with First Nations and other non-Western and feminist philosophies and ignoring its racialized assumptions. Even posthumanist philosophy, despite awareness of the deeply entangled, relational and porous nature of humanness, has tended to position people as very different from and superior to other living things (Aloi, 2022; TallBear, 2015; Todd, 2016).

The One Health approach that has emerged in public health scholarship and practice is beginning to adopt recognition of the more-than-human dimensions of human and planetary wellbeing. It encourages a broader ecological focus, incorporating all living things and features of the natural environment in its purview. The One Health position, led by animal health and infectious disease experts, has already recognized that human and animal health and wellbeing are entangled and relational with that of the environment. Proponents argue for human and veterinary medicine to be more closely intertwined, as they were prior to the early twentieth century (Mwangi et al., 2016). Animal ethics scholars are only beginning to acknowledge other living and non-living entities as part of a One Health approach (Coghlan et al., 2021). Critics in fields such as anthropology and postcolonial studies have argued that, while animal agency in planetary health is acknowledged in One Health discourses and practices, there is still some way to go to move beyond the human-centric focus that many proponents continue to adopt, led by existing ideas and attitudes to other animals expressed in both veterinary science and public health. Indeed, this approach has been criticized for its Western and colonial viewpoint and lack of acknowledgement of the non-Western traditional worldviews of human–non-human relations that have always recognized human health and wellbeing as entangled with other beings, the ecosystem and the environment (Baquero et al., 2021; Wolf, 2015).

More-than-human perspectives adopt an approach to understanding the nature of human existence in a way that decentres the human and challenges post-Enlightenment Western concepts. Any existing notion of human exceptionalism, and the conceptualization of the human body/self that positions it as bounded, individual and autonomous, are exposed for their simplistic assumptions. More-than-human worldviews see human bodies and selves as inextricably intertwined with non-human agents. These agents include other animals and living things, together with features of place and space such as geological formations and bodies of water. The human-built environment and human-made objects are also included in these more-than-human assemblages of which people are part. These perspectives offer a more relational philosophical approach to human–animal interactions which acknowledges that people can never be individuated and autonomous from other living creatures and from the material dimensions of place and space: the sky, the wind, rain, sun and snow, the earth, the solar system, the seas and waterways, rocks and mountains. They emphasize the connections and entanglements of the lives and bodies of animals with each other, together with humans and other ecological elements. The concept of relational agency espoused in more-than-human philosophy acknowledges the intersections and relationships not only between humans and other humans when they assemble, but also between humans and nonhumans, and nonhumans with each other. Agencies are viewed as never pre-existing or properties of actors (human or nonhuman). Rather, they come into being when assemblages gather, and, as such, are motile and emergent rather than fixed. These are flat rather than hierarchical ontologies.

More-than-human perspectives continue to be central to the cosmologies of Indigenous / First Nations peoples and many contemporary cultures of the Global South. Diverse spiritual or cosmological beliefs in non-Western and First Nations' cultures already position animals as part of more-than-human systems. North American First Nations theorist Kim TallBear (2015: 234) has pointed out that 'indigenous peoples have never forgotten that nonhumans are agential beings engaged in social relations that profoundly shape human lives'. First Nations cultures broadly share an animist perspective on non-human entities and agents – whether they are part of natural ecologies or are directly human-made – that view them as possessing liveliness, spirit or animacy in ways that contemporary Western cultures tend to deny. TallBear (2015: 234) puts it this way: '"Objects" and "forces" such as stones, thunder, or stars are known within our ontologies to be sentient and knowing persons.' Relationality is the source of knowledge (how the world is known) and the life force that animates agents, supporting and nourishing life (Hernández et al., 2020; TallBear, 2015; Todd, 2016; Tynan, 2021).

For Australian First Nations people, the concept of Country encapsulates these vibrant gatherings of humans and nonhumans. As First Nations Australian Lauren Tynan (2021: 597) defines it: 'Country inhabits all relationality and is used widely across Australia to describe how all land is Aboriginal land, Aboriginal Country; Country is agentic and encompasses everything from ants, memories, humans, fire, tides and research.' Country connects humans to systems of knowledges and law that can never be human-centric. In cosmologies such as those held by the North American Plains Cree culture, these ontologies are often shifting: objects or places may move between animacy and inanimacy at certain times or places or when other agents, including humans, assemble with them. Regardless of animacy status, all agents are considered to be included within the circle of kinship (Lewis et al., 2018; Tynan, 2021).

Ecofeminist perspectives also adopt an intersectional approach that positions other living entities, both animals and plants, as cultural beings, enmeshed in social, political and cultural systems of meaning and practice (Irni, 2020). Scholars such as Val Plumwood (2002) and Greta Gaard (2015) bring together concerns from feminist and queer theory and species justice to examine the multiplicities of forms of economic exploitation and violence that affect both animals and humans who are positioned as Other to mainstream norms of identity and embodiment. The multispecies studies perspective espoused in environmental humanities focuses specifically on the emergent and dynamic nature of assemblages of human, animal and other species, exploring the connections and vitalities that emerge when multiple species come together (Tsing, 2015; Van Dooren et al., 2016). Such a perspective can begin from the microbiological level, by recognizing our bodies as a multispecies assemblage composed of millions of microbes that come together to configure our personal microbiomes: none of which is the same as that of any other individual, and none of which remains the same from moment to moment (Greenhough et al., 2020; Wolf, 2015).

Similarly, feminist materialist scholars, including Karen Barad (2007), Rosi Braidotti (2016) and Jane Bennett (2010), acknowledge the vitality of things. They conceptualize vitality as flows of forces and intensities across human and nonhuman encounters, connecting people and things. Barad (2007) describes these relational encounters as 'intra-actions', in which capacities, connections and agencies are opened up. These assemblages configure forces that are relational, dynamic, and contingent on the time and space through and in which humans move, and the other humans, living creatures and objects with which they come into contact.

More-than-human scholarship has devoted attention to identifying and understanding the vitalities, relational connections and affective forces that are generated when humans come together with digital technologies. Feminist technoscience philosopher Donna Haraway has played a prominent role in contributing to scholarship on the nature of human–nonhuman assemblages. Her writings on what she describes as 'naturecultures' recognize the blurred boundaries not only between nature and culture, but also between humans and other agents (Haraway and Goodeve, 2000). In her work on the metaphorical figure of the cyborg, Haraway (1985) draws attention to the idea that human ontologies must be understood as multiple and dynamic rather than fixed and essential, emerging through relational encounters. The cyborg metaphor encapsulates this idea in relation not only to human–technology assemblages, but to any interaction of humans with nonhumans: including living things. This perspective provides a basis for thinking through the emergent ontologies of animal–human–digital assemblages.

In later writings, Haraway (2003) used the term 'companion species' to describe the relationships that the human species has with other animal species and with technologies. In her book *The Companion Species Manifesto* (2003), Haraway wrote extensively about her relationship with her dog. For Haraway, humans are companion species with the nonhumans alongside which they live and engage, each species learning from and influencing the other, co-evolving. Animals are always part of our multispecies embodied and kinship relations (whether they live in our houses or not). She does not approve of the common conceptualization of companion animals such as dogs, cats and rabbits as 'fur babies' or ersatz children or other ways of anthropomorphizing or infantilizing animals. In Haraway's view, animals are companions, but they are not humans – and nor should they be treated as commodities or possessions for the amusement or comfort of humans. Haraway's main point is that kin relations with other animals are as important as those with other humans. Understanding this broadening of kin relationships helps us to reconceptualize our position in naturecultures and see the world otherwise (Haraway, 2016).

In more recent scholarship, Haraway (2015) describes companion species as 'post-cyborg entities', acknowledging the development of her thinking since her original cyborg exegesis. She also now refers to herself not as a 'posthumanist' but as a 'compost-ist', adopting the metaphor of compost to describe the living, moving assemblages that comprise human–nonhuman gatherings and intra-actions. For Haraway (2016), the metaphor of 'compost' sums up the manifold vibrant complexities that are represented in these assemblages of humans–nonhumans. Compost is comprised of all kinds of biological matter, including microorganisms and animals such as worms and insects, but can also include fragments of human-made items such as plastics: all cycling through the processes of decay and renewal. Human bodies themselves become part of the biosphere when they are dead and are broken down into compost by bacteria and other living creatures.

Drawing on these more-than-human understandings of distributed agency and embodiment, digital technologies and digital data can also be viewed as companion species contributing to the 'compost' of life (Lupton, 2019b; Lupton et al., 2022). Humans' and animals' embodied experiences are entangled in lively animal–human–digital assemblages. These dynamic encounters and exchanges configure complex and ever-changing interconnected natureculture worlds of humans and other animals with viruses, bacteria, fungi, parasitic worms and other microorganisms situated in place, space and time. Working together, humans, animals, digital technologies and other agents intra-act to generate affective intensities and agential capacities, inspiring and enabling action, knowledge and other responses.

Cultivating attentiveness and responsiveness

Bioethicists and moral philosophers often position themselves as disinterested, disembodied and rational agents, engaging in logical application of normative judgements. The standpoint and acculturated context of the scholar who is making judgements about the ethical dimensions of human practice is often invisible, as they present themselves as adopting a universalist moral stance. This is a 'view from nowhere', in Haraway's (1988) words. In contrast, a more-than-human approach highlights 'the view from somewhere' and emphasizes the always tenuous, situated and dynamic nature of ethical appraisal. This perspective calls attention to the intertwining of ethics with ontologies and epistemologies, as captured in Barad's (2007) formulation of onto-ethico-epistemology. Just as more-than-human theory recognizes a distributed and emergent concept of agency, it also positions ethics as distributed and emergent rather than fixed or normative. Scholars and researchers – including bioethicists and moral ethicists – are positioned as part of research assemblages situated in time and place. They will always inevitably hold a partial perspective when considering ethical issues (Barad, 2007; Haraway, 1988).

Abandoning the traditional emphasis in animal ethics and bioethics on hierarchies of sentience in animal species goes a long way to developing a more responsive and attentive ethical position. Relationships of mutual respect and reciprocity underpin First Nations peoples' worldviews on understanding and engagement with nonhumans. People are expected to consider the wellbeing of nonhumans in everything that they do, behaving responsibly to all forms of life (Hernández et al., 2020; Lewis et al., 2018; Robinson, 2014; Tynan, 2021). Together with ecofeminisms, feminist materialisms and environmental humanities, these philosophies already acknowledge the agencies, intelligences and vitalities of all nonhuman entities, including but not limited to other animals. Such approaches recognize

that settlers, capitalists and colonialists have historically exploited, enslaved and murdered other humans
in the interests of achieving wealth and power, treating
marginalized social groups as Other and less-than-
human resources, just as they have positioned animals
as inferior to humans and deserving little respect or
protection (Belcourt, 2015; Gaard, 2015; Lewis et al.,
2018; Plumwood, 2002).

As noted earlier in this chapter, elements of a more-
than-human worldview were characteristic of Western
cultures before the Enlightenment. They have not completely disappeared in Global North societies, but have
been pushed to the margins in dominant representations, ideals and practices of 'the human'. Nonetheless,
a notable intensification of thought and movements in
the West towards recuperating the more-than-human
perspective is evident across cultures of environmental
and climate activism and critiques of human exceptionalism. Posthuman philosopher Cary Wolfe (2010: 135),
for example, argues for developing a 'trans-species affinity' that involves humans acknowledging that they are
animals characterized by engagements with the world
that are part of a 'generalized animal sensorium'. He
argues that this affinity goes beyond recognition of the
speciesism identified by Peter Singer and his followers
by avoiding the human-centric appraisal of rights. All
lifeforms are part of trans-species entanglements and are
therefore in the field of ethical responsiveness. Similarly,
a central interest in multispecies studies is asking what
is at stake when attention is paid to these intersections
and enactments, how 'species' might be defined, what
the implications are for ethical and caring relationships
between humans and other species, and what account-
abilities need to be acknowledged (Van Dooren et al.,
2016).

Indigenous, First Nations and other non-Western philosophies adopt a very different moral perspective on such issues as hunting, killing and eating animals. There are ages-old knowledges, rituals and ceremonies that highlight the respect and ethical commitment that humans have towards other animals and living things – including those animals that people kill and consume. For example, for the Mi'kmaq, a First Nations people who traditionally inhabited the eastern coast of North America, animals are conceptualized as siblings and persons, rational beings who live and think for themselves. It is believed that animals willingly sacrifice themselves to become food through a reciprocal and respectful relationship with humans as part of a broad web of interdependence. Humans pay respect to the animals they kill and consume through rituals that honour their sacrifice. Importantly, the Mi'kmaq are careful to kill only as many animals as they need for subsistence, avoiding exploitation of the animals' generosity in offering themselves. Indeed, it is through their relationships with other animals and living things that the Mi'kmaq see themselves as becoming human (Robinson, 2014).

The emphasis on sentience in animal ethics is a limited perspective on the agencies and capacities of any form of life. Recent scholarship on the amazingly complex systems of plant, animal, fungi, soil and microbiota, as they work together symbiotically to create and sustain life (Abram, 2021; Sheldrake, 2020), demonstrates that human interpretations and assessments of nonhuman cognition, consciousness, feeling and agency are rudimentary at best. Academic research on animal, plant, fungi, viral and microorganism 'intelligence' – that is, their sophisticated ways of communicating and actively engaging in complex ecological networks – is still emerging, but it is becoming clear that there are manifold dimensions of this nonhuman 'intelligence' that we have no way of noticing or comprehending. Indeed, the contributions of the cooperating colonies of microorganisms that contribute to the microbiome, contributing to human health and functioning, are only just beginning to be recognized and explored (Greenhough et al., 2020; Hinchliffe, 2022).

Legal thought in both the Global North and Global South is beginning to recognize agents such as bodies of water as living beings with rights. As long ago as 2008, the Ecuador Constitution enshrined the rights of nature. Similar moves to recognize animal rights have been initiated around the globe. New Zealand has legally recognized the rights of the Whanganui River, the Ganges and its tributaries have been recognized in India, and Colombia has ratified the rights of the Atrato River as part of Rights of Nature ordinances in courts and legislatures (Gellers, 2021). In Australia, the Yarra River in Melbourne was recognized as an integrated living natural entity through an Act of Parliament in 2017, with its Indigenous name, Birrarung, acknowledged in the legislation. The Birrarung Act is written partly in local First Nations language, and refers to the ancestral beings in Dreaming stories that have held the river and its kin in balance (Emmanouil, 2021).

A more-than-human perspective, therefore, takes a much more dynamic and contextual approach to ethics than is typically espoused in the animal ethics and bioethics literature. It seeks to uncover the ethical implications of the entanglements between humans and nonhumans, the material-discursive relational connections between agents, the distribution of agencies, and the affective and multisensory dimensions of these phenomena. More-than-human theory positions justice and rights as more-than-human, trans-species and transnational. For

Rosi Braidotti, this is a 'nomadic ethics' responding to 'nomadic subjectivity' (2006: 4). Nomadic ethics recognizes the mutability and complexity of identities as they are mediated globally and technologically, challenging the idea of moral universalism. Braidotti (2006) sees a move towards nomadic ethics as embracing relativism in the quest for new, more creative and better accounts of being-in-the-world, including a heightened awareness of and sensitivity to people's connectedness to other humans and to nonhumans.

Such an approach can be described as 'queering' relations of care, or questioning the dominant norms and assumptions that underpin such relations (Irni, 2020). Tsz Man Chan (2018) uses the term 'postanimalism' to describe these perspectives on nonhuman animals: an approach that abandons not only the attempt to position humans as separate and distinct from other animals, but also any ordering of species based on factors such as their assumed sentience. For cultural ecologist and geophilosopher David Abram, developing what he calls a 'wild ethics' is vital to healing the planet. Abram argues not only that humans need to recognize that we inhabit a common world with other beings and that we are part of a community of more-than-human living subjects, but that our animal nature needs to be re-established. Wild ethics, for Abram (2021: 50), does not rest on a humanistic and rationalist set of rules. Instead, it involves developing 'a simple humility toward others – an attentive openness not just toward other persons but also toward the inexhaustible otherness of the manifold beings that compose this earthly world'.

Many thorny questions and issues are raised about how humans digitize and datafy animals. In thinking through the relational and agential dimensions of animal–human–digital encounters, a more-than-human approach can begin to incorporate these approaches to ethics. It can acknowledge and address the deeper affective, multisensory and relational dimensions of humans' and other animals' encounters with and enactments of these things, and the ways in which technological affordances come together with bodily affordances to open or close agential capacities in complex, dynamic and multiple ways. Adopting an attentive and responsive approach to care involves recognizing both the benefits and harms that digitization and datafication can have for more-than-human flourishing and wellbeing, including the implications for interspecies relational connections. This includes devoting attention to the specificities and historicities of how digital technologies are designed, promoted and used – especially as the conditions of use are constantly changing when new technologies are promoted and introduced into the worlds of animals. In the following chapters, these issues are examined in detail.

2
Animal Enthusiasts, Activism and Politics in Digital Media

Since the early years of the internet, websites, discussion forums and social media platforms have offered opportunities for wild animal enthusiasts and activists – as well as people involved professionally or informally in the care and husbandry of farm animals, rescued or protected animals, wild animals and domestic animals – to share their passion and know-how with each other. This chapter examines modes of digitizing and datafying animals, with particular attention to the ways that communities of knowledge creation and sharing are generated and maintained, how competing political tensions surface and are expressed, and the circulation of affect in and through these encounters of humans with each other and with animals.

Wild animal enthusiast networks and citizen science initiatives

As part of the digital sharing economy, animals are often the topic of shared interests online. This includes animal enthusiasts, who bond with each other online about their specific interests in classes or species of animals.

Such sites include those for birders, who share images they have captured on their devices of the varieties of birdlife they have spotted in their environs, remarking on its distinctive features, its rarity or the beauty of its colourings. Birdwatching blogs, Facebook groups and online guides are available for bird identification. Twitter provides many opportunities for birders to share their sightings. Some of these accounts use bots to detect automatically images of birds and share them: @BirdPerHour and @_everybird are examples. There are a series of similar bot accounts on Twitter that regularly share images of other wild animals for followers, including @PossumEveryHour, @racoonhourly, @HourlyLynxes and @gatorsdaily (for alligators).

Citizen science initiatives using digital sensors and other digitized data collection techniques have contributed to the amassing of databases about phenomena such as the environmental effects of pollution, localized climate change impacts, loss of species diversity and efforts to regenerate cleared land (Gabrys, 2019). Examples of citizen science initiatives to generate data about wild animals to contribute to conservation efforts include US-based Cornell University's eBird platform, described by the researchers who established it as helping people to 'Discover a new world of birding'. Using the eBird platform and associated phone app, birders are encouraged to upload information about their avian sightings and to join the online birding community by sharing these data with other enthusiasts. This information is archived and processed by the eBird developers to contribute to 'eBird science' outputs such as creating data visualizations showing different avian species' habitats, and breeding and migration patterns. The eBird website notes that these data can be downloaded by eBird users for their own research as well as contributing to initiatives such as conservation, species management and habitat protection and the development of regulation and policies for the protection of birds globally (Cornell Lab of Ornithology, 2022).

MammalWeb is a similar platform for citizen science. The platform is a collaboration between Durham University and Durham Wildlife Trust in the UK. Digital cameras are used, together with motion sensors, to capture images of wild mammals (such as badgers, deer, foxes and rabbits) moving around their habitats. Citizens living in the UK and Continental Europe are invited to set up such a 'camera trap' in their local area and upload the images to the platform, and also to help the researchers identify the animals captured in the images. This information is used by the research team to gain more knowledge about the distribution and numbers of these animals, their health and responses to environmental changes over time (MammalWeb, 2022).

Some of these projects take place in cityscapes. The 'Shazam for Bats' project, based in a London park as part of a Smart Sustainable District programme, is one such initiative (Hudson-Smith et al., 2019). The project positions bats and their behaviours as a way of monitoring the health of the environment in which they (and humans) live. A network of fifteen 'smart bat' monitors was installed across the park in different micro-habitats. These Echo Box monitors work on the principles of the popular Shazam app, used globally to identify music. Each Echo Box was equipped with an ultrasonic microphone, which recorded the soundscape of the place. These sonic data were processed by turning them into a visual image (a spectrogram), which was scanned using machine learning software to identify the bat species most likely to have made each call. These data are provided to park ecologists to assist them in plotting seasonal shifts and variations in weather conditions that influence the bats' habits, together with the effects of such human-made technologies as street lighting strategies.

While the portrayal of wild animals online as part of enthusiast networks can promote conservation efforts, they can also result in harmful consequences for these animals. The trafficking of wild animals for sale as pets or for food and medical use has become a major problem worldwide. Online forums, social media platforms and messaging apps are important media for communication by members of illegal wildlife trading economies. It has been estimated that 38 million wild animals each year have been captured from their natural habitats in the rainforests of Brazil alone, and then trafficked to other countries for private zoos, as pets or for human consumption or use in medicinal treatments. The threat to these animals' welfare and to local and global biodiversity is enormous (Wyatt et al., 2022).

TikTok has recently become a digital space where wild animals feature heavily. The top animal accounts in terms of earnings identified in BuzzBingo's 'Pet TikTok Rich List 2021' (BuzzBingo, 2022) is headed by the @kodyantle account, with close to 22 million followers and almost 300 million likes. This account is run by animal trainer and star of the Netflix docu-series *Tiger King*, Kody Antle. It features his tiger and the other exotic animals with which he lives at his family's wildlife park in South Carolina, USA. The videos show Antle feeding and playing with the animals and often copying their behaviour (swinging on rafters with a chimpanzee, swimming with a tiger). As demonstrated by the popularity of Antle's TikTok account, exotic pets are admired on that platform. This popularity has been identified as potentially problematic by experts in animal welfare, who are concerned that people following the accounts may attempt to take on the care of a wild animal themselves without realizing the implications and difficulties. Foxes, servals (a wild cat native to Africa), racoons and kinkajous (a mammal from the racoon family that lives in tropical rainforest habitats in Central America, also known as a 'honey bear') are among the most popular on TikTok. There are communities of wild animal owners on this platform who share advice on how best to care for these creatures. However, as these animals are wild rather than domesticated, they can become difficult to manage in captivity as they grow older. Animal experts on TikTok warn others against purchasing these animals, emphasizing that they are not appropriate pets. Some owners who post TikToks of their wild animals have been accused of placing them or other people into dangerous situations simply to attract views and likes (Faheid, 2021).

Veganism, vegetarianism and animal activism

In his analysis of animals in popular culture, Randy Malamud (2012) points out that anodyne entertaining or spectacular portrayals of animals historically far outnumber those that show the realities of human cruelty to animals: their living conditions in industrial farming contexts; their slaughter and dismemberment as part of hunting activities or the meat industry. It is here that animal activist groups and organizations have stepped in, strategically employing often extremely confronting images as part of drawing public attention to these issues. There are manifold examples of animal rights, anti-animal-cruelty and vegetarian and vegan activism groups online. Their activism sometimes intersects with broader environmental sustainability and climate change activism, as well as more specifically food-related activism that is directed at ensuring that food is healthy, free from contaminants and ethically produced.

Since the advent of the internet, such groups have been highly successful in using websites, discussion forums and both dedicated and mainstream social media platforms to draw attention to their cause (Lupton, 2018). They coalesce as 'issue publics': groups that conduct public discussions around specific topics that are often political or contentious, often using 'hashtag activism' to organize themselves (Rodak, 2020). Such groups have also been described as 'digital counter publics' who are challenging taken-for-granted attitudes and practices in the public sphere with the intention of changing public opinion (Wonneberger et al., 2021).

People who adhere to vegetarian and vegan diets have used social media, video-sharing platforms and online discussion forums for decades as a way of supporting each other and providing inspiration and recipes for meals (Braun and Carruthers, 2020). In my online survey, I asked whether respondents ever looked at animal-related content on the internet or apps for dietary, political or activism purposes (e.g. veganism or animal activism content). Almost half (46 per cent) said that they did and went on to provide details. Some people reported mostly focusing on researching plant-based practices and recipes:

> I look for vegetarian recipes online as my partner and I are trying to reduce our meat consumption.

> I find vegan and vegetarian recipes and information on Instagram.

Most of the other respondents who answered this question, however, were more interested in using the internet to find and share content related to political veganism or vegetarianism, and other topics concerning animal activism, rescue and conservation efforts, environmentalism or anti-cruelty initiatives:

> I follow some vegan accounts on Instagram and also the accounts of some people that rescue animals. I like seeing rescued animals getting a better life and learning how to further contribute to the cause of animal rights.

> I follow a farm that grows lambs and calves as part of a local, eco-friendly farm. The animals are treated humanely, and I have also visited the farm myself as I believe in small-scale humane farming practices.

> I used to be vegetarian for several years and I would check online, just Google, about products made of or tested on animals. I still care about the testing although I stopped being vegetarian every day.

Many vegetarians and vegans express strong affective responses on social media and in visual media to the idea of eating animal flesh or consuming other animal-derived products, such as eggs and dairy foods. When I searched for GIFs and memes about meat eating, I noted that people who eat meat are often portrayed in these media as grotesque, greedy and animal-like in their behaviour, stuffing large portions of meat or chicken drumsticks into their mouths and smearing their faces with the food. On Instagram, a social media platform known principally for its beautiful and highly stylized visual aesthetics, particularly in relation to food (Lupton, 2018), animal liberation accounts such as Animal Liberation Front (with close to 58,000 followers) present 'ugly' and confronting images of animals being mistreated. One popular animal rights influencer, @alf_sweden (with over 78,000 followers), includes in

her feed manipulated images showing such bizarre jux-
tapositions as a group of smiling young people sitting
around a dinner table with dismembered animal car-
casses lying on the table instead of cooked food (and a
mother figure standing at the head of the table proudly
bearing an uncooked pig's head on a platter).

In contrast, vegan Instagram accounts tend to focus
on recipes and attractive photos of vegan food adhering
to the 'food porn' and 'clean eating' aesthetics, demonstrating a move away from ethical veganism to a dietary
practice that has more emphasis on health and wellbeing (Braun and Carruthers, 2020; Lupton, 2018). As
this suggests, not all vegetarians and vegans are animal
rights or anti-cruelty activists or prefer animal-free diets
for ethical reasons. Some are predominantly motivated
by health or environmental sustainability concerns.
Social media influencers – typically, young, slim and
usually white women – have often drawn on vegetarian
and vegan principles to promote 'clean eating' lifestyles.
It is notable that creative cuisine and offering delicious
or inexpensive vegan recipes, together with messages
about body positivity, rather than explicit references
to animal rights or wellbeing, dominate the content of
the top vegan YouTubers (several of whom are men)
(Smith, 2020).

Alternatively, cute imagery and humour are frequently used in visual media such as GIFs and memes
to contribute to and support communities of vegans
and vegetarians. One example is a meme that shows
three men in a car, with one yelling and another placing his fingers in his ears. The wording reads: 'Meat
eater's [sic] reaction when you tell them the truth about
the meat industry'. GIFs and memes showing smiling
cartoon fruit and vegetables and the words 'Proud to be
vegan', 'Eat vegan' or 'Eat your veggies', or that show

baby animals with the words 'Friends, not food', 'Vegan for the animals', 'Love all animals' and 'I just want to be loved', or calves with their mothers and the text 'They belong together', draw on sentimentality and cute imagery to inspire positive feelings about vegetarianism and veganism. These latter styles of representation contribute to the framing of ethical vegan and vegetarian eating practices as feminized practices that are driven by affection for the kinds of animals that are slaughtered for human consumption. Any direct condemnation of meat eating is absent by design, replaced by warm intimate feelings of care and conviviality for these animals.

Social media platforms offer many special interest groups for advocating against animal cruelty. Some forms of digitization and datafication can be used by humans to both identify and bear witness to the suffering of animals (Frichot, 2022). These actions are particularly evident among animal activist groups and organizations which employ social media accounts to distribute information about the cruelty inflicted by people on animals, often accompanied by compellingly disturbing and graphic images of the animals being mistreated. The suffering of these animals is evident in their wounded, bloodied or distorted embodiment, and often also the characteristics of their spatial surroundings: factory-farmed fowl, for example, kept squashed together in cages with little room for movement. These are examples of animals bearing witness, facilitated by the affordances of digital media. Their bodies bear witness to the human-inflicted suffering, and these images are used by humans to bear witness to the conditions under which they live and die.

Major animal liberation organizations have been established, with strong social media presences across numerous platforms. On Twitter, for example, The

Humane League, We Animals Media, Animal Justice, Mercy for Animals, Vegan Future, Vegan Society and Farm Sanctuary run accounts with tens or hundreds of thousands of followers. Their visual media include explicitly political content, such as photographs of animals in distress, people engaging in animal activism protest activities or calls to sign online petitions, references to celebrity activists or vegans (British musician Paul McCartney and US Olympian athlete Carl Lewis, for example) and scientists who work on cruelty-free food products. These Twitter accounts also feature promotions of animal-free meals, snacks and beverages, travel guides, and products such as housing materials, clothing and footwear, cosmetics, skincare, and vitamin supplements to support vegan diets. This content, therefore, combines a rich mixture of older-style political activism and animal liberation messages with celebrity, wellness and commodity culture.

Vegan Outreach is one such organization, with a high social media presence across numerous platforms. It boasts almost a million 'likes' on Facebook and also offers an associated website, together with Twitter, Instagram and YouTube accounts. Vegan Outreach is described as 'a leading international non-profit on a mission to end animal suffering'. The most recent content offered when I reviewed its website (Vegan Outreach, 2022) included details about initiatives in India to 'veganize' meals offered by restaurants and cafeterias in that country, calling for donations to support work such as this; videos about how to make vegan food (for example, vegan chocolate cake); images of people cuddling or feeding baby animals; inspiring quotations from famous animal-lovers or scientists such as Jane Goodall; and calls for 'more empathy' to be directed towards animals.

It is mostly farm animals that feature on the Vegan Outreach Facebook page. Viewers are requested to support and protect these creatures by eschewing eating animal flesh and products. The page shows appealing images of piglets, chicks and calves, together with statements such as 'The animals are counting on us to spread veganism and bring an end to the violence they endure', 'They want to live', 'They need their mother's milk [showing calves suckling]' and 'I'm a baby, not bacon.' The link to animal liberation discourses and ideology (chapter 1) is made clear in such statements as 'Our work is to end speciesism and the violence that comes from it.' In addition to the baby farm animal images, there is also more confronting content such as photographs of chickens in factory-farming conditions ('This is what hens endure so we can eat their eggs'). These images and words mostly rely on an idealized and nostalgic portrayal of the 'natural' life that farm animals 'should' live without human intervention. The focus is on motivating people to take up veganism, donate to the cause and spread the word: the website's main message is 'Violence towards animals is happening now. And you can help stop it' (Vegan Outreach, 2022).

PETA (People for the Ethical Treatment of Animals) is among the most well-known and largest animal rights organizations. It has long had a strong social media and website presence to draw attention to its cause and attract new members. PETA's Facebook community page has 6 million 'likes' and there are over 1 million Twitter followers, with the hashtag #EndSpeciesism again gesturing towards the language of the animal liberation movement. Similar content is shared across the two platforms and on the PETA website, including confronting images of dead or maimed animals or those in distress, together with vegan recipes and winsome baby animal photos. Farm animals again feature, but other mammals who are being badly treated also appear regularly in the Facebook and Twitter feeds. The plight of kittens, rabbits and puppies bred for pet shops, rabbits and rodents used in scientific research or product testing, hunted wild animals and those killed in the fur trade, as well as wildlife captured for zoos, circuses, medicines or human consumption, is publicized across PETA's online accounts.

As is the case with the Vegan Outreach digital media content, PETA devotes a high level of attention to humanizing the animals it features and attempting to provoke affects of protectiveness, concern and care for them. There are frequent references to 'babies' and their 'mothers', and the separation that is forced on them by humans. The tagline for its website makes a direct appeal to viewers not to objectify animals or see them as possessions: 'Animals are not ours . . . to experiment on, eat, wear, use for entertainment, or abuse in any other way' (PETA, 2022a). It is notable, however, that the vast majority of animals featured in PETA's online content are furry, cuddly mammals, with the exception of some species of birds bred for consumption or kept as pets and limited reference to reptiles and amphibians in the exotic pet trade.

Contesting veganism and animal activism

While animal rights activism organizations and their supporters are clearly achieving high levels of presence and attention online, there are also efforts to counter their messages with competing perspectives. Vegan and vegetarian content creators are often made fun of or even subjected to hate speech and trolling by other internet and social media users. Some GIFs and memes are designed to counter anti-meat-eating discourses by directly challenging them. Examples include a meme showing a piglet and the words 'I don't always eat meat, but when I do, it's bacon', and another using a close-up photo of a slab of raw red meat, with the text 'Dear vegans, I killed this cow because it was eating your food. You're welcome!'. In these digital media, veganism and vegetarianism are typically presented as feminine 'hippy' practices, involving young women who are sentimental about animals and prone to lecturing others. Memes conveying these sentiments include one showing a young white woman with blonde dreadlocks and facial piercings with the words 'Why did the vegan cross the road? To tell somebody else that she's a vegan.'

These words and images together portray the typical vegan as a young woman who adheres to counter-cultural practices and bodily appearance: far from the mainstream food consumer. Anti-vegan GIFs and memes can be even more misogynistic: for example, a meme showing a woman being held upside down and forced to eat grass by a man, as if she were a lawnmower, with the text 'Pros of having a vegan girlfriend'. Such representations draw on and reproduce long-held discourses and practices in Western cultures that gender red meat as a typically masculine food, representing strength, aggression and virility, while a mostly or solely vegetarian diet is presented as adhering to normative femininity, conveying the meanings of passivity and weakness (Adams, 2010; Lupton, 1996). Women's bodies themselves are often portrayed as 'meat' in Western food cultures, including the depiction of them as helpless animals to be subjugated, and sexual objectification of them as things for the use and pleasure of men (Adams, 2010; Gaard, 2015).

These gendered discourses and practices are prominent in another example of misogyny coming together with pro-meat-eating cultures on the internet: YouTube videos which advocate for the excessive consumption of meat as a spectacle of masculinist prowess. The Epic Meal Time YouTube channel, created by Canadian male YouTubers in 2012 and now with 7 million followers and hosting hundreds of videos, is one particularly grotesque portrayal of such hyper-consumption and 'bro' culture' (Lupton, 2020a). The videos feature these men literally throwing together huge meals made of meat products (bacon always features heavily), such as giant hamburgers, burritos, pizzas and 'the world's largest lasagne'. As they slam food down and arrange it, these men constantly comment on how much they enjoy consuming meat. Aggression (thinly disguised as humour) towards both the meat itself and to people who eschew meat eating is frequently emphasized as part of a macho portrayal of men's fervent desire for meat. One example is the 'Meat Tank' video, published in 2013. It begins with the YouTubers declaiming that they are fighting back against health food and for their 'right to eat meat'. They begin to construct their 'meat tank' dish, a meat loaf made of bacon, meat balls, salami and minced meat. As these men put the dish together, they comment on how they are 'sickos' who enjoy 'smashing eggs' and 'squishing the meat'. Several such videos feature references that sexualize meat products (they comment that 'this is pretty much sex' as they handle meat in the 'Meat Tank' video) or make direct references that compare women's bodies to meat. In these highly gendered social imaginaries, it is 'natural' for 'real' men to enjoy practices such as handling and consuming animal flesh in the same way as they desire to make use of the bodies of women.

In a very different approach, farmers and the meat industry have capitalized on the bucolic aesthetics of the classic 'nature' image by engaging in attempts to refute and allay growing public concerns about animal welfare on farms. For example, Swedish milk producers have used Facebook and Instagram accounts to present 'farming fantasies' depicting fairy-tale imagery of 'happy cows' and friendly cow–human relations on dairy farms. These practices are attempts to generate affects of intimacy and conviviality in milk consumers, thereby countering activist criticisms by presenting milk and the cows who produce it as cruelty-free and symbolically pure and wholesome. In this context, the cows not only are working to produce milk for human consumption, but also are performing as emotional labourers on the behalf of the dairy industry marketing initiatives, making people feel better about exploiting their bodies (Linné, 2016).

Similarly, an analysis of Twitter content created and shared by farmers (Riley and Robertson, 2021) found that farming practices documented in these tweeted images and texts conformed to a strongly positive representation. The farmers portrayed life on the land as hard but satisfying and fulfilling work, with many rosy images shared of rolling green fields and contented creatures enjoying their life on the farm. Farmers documenting their work lives on Twitter emphasized the contribution they are making to society, such as rising before dawn every day of the year to milk the cows so that other people can have milk for their breakfast. The cultural fantasy of rural life is perpetuated on farming Twitter, with farmers attempting to demonstrate their care for the welfare of their animals. While these tweets generally make little direct mention of animal activists' or publics' concerns about farm animals' welfare and living conditions, they indirectly operate to challenge and refute these discourses.

The ideal of 'happy meat' on Instagram is a similar portrayal, referring to animal flesh that is 'sold with a story' about the serenely natural lives enjoyed by cattle, chickens and pigs that are raised for human consumption (Buddle, 2022: 166). Some meat producers in countries such as Australia and the USA who eschew methods of intensive farming create Instagram content depicting farm animals destined for slaughter as experiencing contented lives and pain-free deaths. This approach conforms to the 'ethical meat' discourse, which has been taken up by some producers and marketers in the attempt to appeal to consumers who may have some moral misgivings about the treatment of animals raised for meat or the environmental impacts of industrial farming. Animal flesh labelled as 'organic', 'free range', 'grass-fed', 'hormone-free' or 'environmentally friendly' is sold under the 'ethical meat' banner (Arcari, 2019). In their Instagram accounts, the 'happy meat' producers provide details of where the animals live and how they are fed, regularly posting images that show the animals grazing in spacious grassy fields. Animals are given specially selected names to help convey the impression that they are treated as individuals with personalities, rather than as things. Images uploaded to Instagram by producers attempting to convey the 'happy meat' aesthetic often show farmers or their young children holding baby animals or standing near them in a field, so as to suggest a sense that the farmers have a close family relationship with, and genuine care for, their animals. Transparency about farm conditions is an important factor in attracting consumers wanting 'ethical meat', safe in the knowledge that the animals experience 'a good life' (Arcari, 2019; Buddle, 2022).

The discourse of 'choice' is often employed by these producers in arguing that, if people choose to eat animal flesh, they can also choose to select only meat that comes from ethical meat producers who treat their animals well. Nonetheless, this transparency stops short at the farm gate. Very few details are provided in these 'happy meat' Instagram accounts about how the animals meet their deaths (Buddle, 2022). Such 'ethics-washing' of meat production does little to alter significantly the relations of domination of animals and the perpetuation of the assumption that humans should continue to breed and raise them solely for the purposes of commodifying killing and consuming them – or what Paula Arcari (2019: 175) refers to as 'the meatification' of chickens, pigs and cattle. Indeed, these 'happy' or 'ethical' meat imaginaries operate to cover over the less acceptable practices that continue to pervade meat production (Arcari, 2019).

Competing cultures: the #sealfies debate

Different activist groups with competing agendas and interests have sometimes directly clashed with each other online. One example is the #sealfies debate that ignited in 2014 between North American Indigenous seal hunters and activists protesting against the killing of these creatures. While the Canadian Inuit activists sought to emphasize Indigenous rights to exercise their cultural traditions in seal hunting, animal rights activists championed the perspective of the seals. Both used the #sealfie hashtag and associated images and text to publicize their causes. The word 'sealfie' drew on the initial 'selfie' term that attracted a massive level of attention when American celebrity and talk show host Ellen DeGeneres used the #selfie hashtag to tweet a photograph she had taken on her smartphone at the Academy Awards, of herself and a group of other celebrities. The image was used by DeGeneres for fund-raising for the Humane Society of America, which actively opposes commercial seal hunting in Canada. The selfie was taken on a Samsung smartphone provided to DeGeneres as a product placement promotion. The company agreed to donate money to a charity of DeGeneres' choice each time the image was retweeted (Knezevic et al., 2018; MacNeil, 2014).

In response to this initiative, Inuit activists took to digital media themselves to challenge the Humane Society's stance on seal hunting. YouTube videos were made that sought to provide cultural context to Canadian First Nations' approach to the practice, and arguing that opposition to it was challenging their human rights. Some Inuit activists adapted the word 'selfie' to 'sealfie', tweeting images showing them wearing or holding clothing and other objects made from seal skins as a way of promoting their work and cultural practices. Posters of these images argued that commercial seal hunting had long been well managed, and that Inuit cultural seal hunting was, by contrast, ethical and humane: a central element of the traditional Inuit way of life. They positioned the Humane Society's response as unnecessary and dismissive of traditional Inuit culture and the food, clothing and economic needs of Inuit people (Knezevic et al., 2018).

An Inuit woman and throat singer performer, Tanya Tagaq, joined in the #sealfie sharing on Twitter, posting a more confronting image: a photo she had taken near her hometown of her baby daughter placed on the ground next to the body of a freshly killed adult seal, with blood seeping from its head after it had been shot. The image provoked high levels of controversy, with anti-seal hunting activists challenging the benign nature of the image. One activist manipulated Tagaq's image to show the baby as skinned as if she had been killed by a hunter (MacNeil, 2014). Other outraged Twitter users asserted that Tagaq did not deserve to have a baby and that her photo was evidence that the Inuits are 'savages' and 'mindless scum shit', with some tweeting that Tagaq's baby should be removed from her care (Knezevic et al., 2018). The resultant debates on Twitter were significant enough to make the #sealfie hashtag trend at one point, with mainstream news media picking up the story and subsequently amplifying the conflict (Knezevic et al., 2018).

This debate brings together several dimensions of digital media in relation to the role of their affordances in the portrayal of animals: the selfie photograph and its now numerous variants, the use of hashtags to share topics and create interest networks, the use of social media platforms for activism efforts, and the interplay of digital media with traditional modes of news media. The nature of the visual images employed in the #sealfie photographs shared on Twitter and the competing claims to 'rights' by the protagonists in the debate, together with the affective power of these images, demonstrate the complexities of the more-than-human dimensions of digital media as they relate to human–animal relationships. Complicating these debates is the blurring of boundaries between the categories of 'human' and 'animal' that have long characterized not only Western colonialist and racist perspectives on people of colour and First Nations peoples, but also Indigenous perspectives on human–animal relationships (chapter 1). For the First Nations people arguing for their right to hunt seals in a culturally appropriate manner, long-held beliefs about the intertwinings of humans and animals and their mutually constitutive relationships means that their rights are consonant with the seals' rights. The Western perspective, as articulated by those opposing the #sealfie discourse and imagery, is that both the practices of seal killing and modes of representation online (especially the image showing the positioning of a human baby next to a dead seal) are 'inhumane' – indeed, 'animalistic'.

The cultural meanings surrounding seals (and particularly baby seals) in Western viewpoints also contribute a powerful affective force to anti-seal discourses. As rounded, soft and cuddly-looking mammals with large eyes and pleading expressions, both adult and infant seals are among the most 'infant human'-appearing. My search of hashtags such as #StopTheSealHunt and #sealhunts (often used together with #animalcruelty) on Twitter revealed many such images, typically accompanied by text that argues for the banning of all seal hunting and compares seals with human mothers and babies. One such example is the post by the Twitter account 'Save Animals & Climate', which shared a photograph of a live adult harp seal next to several dead, skinned seals lying in blood-stained snow, together with the words 'Imagine its your Child – thousands of crying Seal Mums who lost their Babies – for human greed, a Jacket or Boots – Seals are living beings – they feel love and Pain' [punctuation and capitalization in the original].

Many other posts using these hashtags promote similar images and rhetoric, drawing attention to the emotions of mother seals in response to their 'babies' being killed and skinned. In an extremely anthropomorphic image, the assumed grief of a female harp seal about the murder of her infant is represented by showing the seal with tears rolling down its face and holding up a portrait ('baby photo') of an infant harp seal. Written in red text below this image are the words 'Stop Canada's shame #sealhunt'. Another Twitter post shares an online petition for people to sign to 'end the seal slaughter in Canada!'. The image illustrating the petition shows an adult and infant harp seal nose-to-nose, with the words 'Mummy I don't want to die, I was just born.' One image on Twitter using the #sealhunt hashtag is a direct appeal to First Nations hunters. It shows a young woman in traditional Indigenous dress and holding a baby being threatened by hunters, drawing an analogy between the woman and a mother seal. Anti-seal-hunting activists have successfully conducted mass media campaigns deploying images of these 'cute' creatures, often shown as murdered and lying in pools of their own blood, starkly highlighted against the snowy environs in which the seals live. Digital media platforms have provided further opportunities over the past two decades to disseminate these images globally. Despite the fact that in Canada far more mink are killed for their furs than infant harp seals, the greater visual and affective appeal of the seals (essentially, their greater baby-like 'cuteness') means that much more attention is paid to their deaths at the hands of humans than to the fate of minks (Knezevic et al., 2018).

Some activists have attempted to incite interest in the impacts of commercial harp seal hunting on the species by making links between seal hunting and climate change – either by using the #climatechange hashtag, or more directly discussing the relationships between the two phenomena. The International Fund for Animal Welfare (IFAW) global not-for-profit organization, for example, covers a broad range of animal welfare issues. A dominant message on the IFAW's website and social media accounts refers to their hashtag #AllTogetherNow. As the website's 'About IFAW' page asserts, the organization focuses on 'helping animals and people thrive together ... Together, we pioneer new and innovative ways to help all species flourish' (IFAW, 2022). Recent IFAW posts emphasize how practices such as seal hunting and culling, combined with climate warming trends (reducing snow and ice cover in harp seals' habitats, making it difficult for female harp seals to give birth and nurture their pups), together threaten the viability of these species. This organization's Twitter account links to articles on its website that invite interested people to read more about these connections. One such article (Fink, 2021) discusses these issues, as well as the spread of misinformation about seals – including the scapegoating of seals by the Government of Canada's Minister of Fisheries in the mid-1990s for reducing fishing stocks due to their predation. At that time, Canadian commercial hunters and fishers were paid to kill seals as a mass culling effort, in a misguided attempt to improve fish stocks. Notably, the strong sentiment about 'cute' cuddly seals seems to have been a more recent affective response, given that not so long ago they were positioned as pests that needed to be killed to protect the economic viability of the Canadian commercial fishing industry.

The digitized animal spectacle

In their analyses of wildlife documentaries, Brett Mills (2010) and Rosemary-Claire Collard (2016) discuss the exploitative and manipulative nature of filmic portrayals of wild animals, noting the relationship between film and violence, and film and affect, in this genre. Mills and Collard show that human exceptionalism underpins wildlife documentaries, as does the exertion of human mastery over animals, their objectification and the rationale for intruding on their lives. It is only because humans have the power to confine animals or enter their natural habitats that such scenes can be captured. In so doing, however, filmmakers are flouting wild animals' desire not to be seen, and potentially interfering with their efforts at food foraging or reproduction. Animals' right to conduct their lives away from the scrutiny and interference of humans is rarely raised as a moral or ethical issue. Indeed, the desire of animals to remain hidden from the human gaze is viewed as a challenge to documentary filmmakers, inciting them to invent ever more intrusive forms of recording details of their lives (Collard, 2016; Mills, 2010). So too, filmmakers' search for the spectacle leads them to over-emphasize aspects of their subjects' activities: for example, by showing scenes of violence against and hunting other animals as occurring far more often than is the case in the animals' lives (Mills, 2010).

There are many resonances, in this analysis of more-than-human and affective dimensions of the wildlife documentary and its treatment of animals, with how we might think about the capturing of visual images and other intimate data about animals described in this chapter. The thrilling affects felt by humans in capturing and viewing the intimate details of the lives and bodies of animals in such films are similar to those experienced in the many forms of digital media used in the interests of animal enthusiast communities, citizen science and political activism. It can be argued that such activities exert an ever widening and often voyeuristic gaze on other creatures, with the vast reams of digitized imagery and other details collected about them not always used to serve the animals' interests. Indeed, while charismatic or cute species may be subjected to digitization and datafication in the interests of their conservation and protection, the monitoring of some wild animals is directly related to attempts to depersonalize these animals in the interests of containment and, in some cases, culling. In all cases, 'nature' – and, by extension, animals – are positioned as phenomena to be observed, managed and controlled by humans (von Essen et al., 2021).

In the emphasis on the 'spectacle' of nature that is often a major attraction of visual digital cultures, animals' bodies, habits and habitats become commodified for humans' consumption. As I have described in this chapter, sometimes activist efforts to bring cruelty against animals to public attention has meant that animals *in extremis* – suffering pain, injury, torture, loss of their infants, cruel death – have received maximum publicity. Here again, while sensitivity to conservation and animal protection may be evoked in human viewers of such spectacles, only a small number of charismatic species are accorded such attentiveness, while others are forgotten and neglected. The more such spectacles rely on the presence of charismatic species, the more conservation efforts are tied to achieving and delivering these dramatic performances of nature (Adams, 2017).

The affordances offered by such direct, intimate and detailed encounters provide additional spectacles and sources of wonder for humans, as they become ever more involved in the private lives (and privations) of animals. These affects can potentially configure convivial multispecies relations (von Essen et al., 2021). However, while humans' fascination can lead to greater empathy with these animals and awareness of threats to their survival posed by humans' actions, there are accompanying risks – including reinforcing the human sense of mastery and control over animals that perpetuates environmental crises and cruelty to animals. The very format of such digital media represents the lives of wild animals as 'invade-able' and fodder for human entertainment, fascination, research or pedagogical purposes (in much the same ways as zoos or circuses) (Mills, 2017). The next chapter examines these issues further, with a focus on how IoT devices, wearable technologies and apps are deployed to generate detailed streams of metricized information about animals' bodies and lives as part of dataveillance strategies.

3
The Quantified Animal and Dataveillance

A growing body of literature in new media and cultural studies has directed attention to the ways people are monitored and measured using digitized self-tracking technologies such as smartphone apps and wearable devices. The term 'dataveillance' is often used to describe how the streams of digital data and the data visualizations generated by these tracking devices can be used for watching people. Now that a plethora of tracking devices and apps are available for conducting dataveillance on animals' bodies and behaviours, similar trends can be observed in human–animal relationships. This chapter will identify the similarities and differences between dataveillance of humans by humans and dataveillance of animals by humans, and consider the implications for how people think, feel and relate to other animals.

Datafication and dataveillance

People move around in data-saturated environments and can wear personalized data-generating devices on their bodies, including not only their smartphones but also objects such as sensor-embedded wristbands, clothing or watches. In distinction from previous technological prostheses, mobile and wearable devices also gather and send out continuous flows of digitized personal information. They have become the repositories of users' communications with others, geolocation information, personal images, biometric information and more. These devices also leak data outwards, transmitting them to computing cloud servers, and are potentially used by third parties for malicious purposes or commercial gain (Lupton, 2016, 2019b). These activities of data generation are commonly referred to as 'the quantified self'. There are five modes of digital monitoring of people: private, pushed, communal, imposed and coerced. Each mode involves different levels of consent, participation and awareness about who is undertaking the digitized monitoring and how these data are being used (Lupton, 2016).

The term 'dataveillance' is often employed to describe how the streams of digital data and the data visualizations generated by these tracking devices can be implemented for watching people. Most scholarly analyses of dataveillance have focused on how digital technologies are used for monitoring, measuring and observing humans' online interactions, their use of digital devices and their movements in place and space (Lupton and Williamson, 2017; Lupton et al., 2022; van Dijck, 2014), as part of what Lyon (2018) refers to as 'the culture of watching'. Researchers in critical data and surveillance studies contributing to this literature have adopted a predominantly negative position on dataveillance of people when it is conducted by third parties, viewing it as overly exploitative, manipulative or coercive (Lyon, 2018; van Dijck, 2014). It has been pointed out that, while some people may voluntarily take up digitized self-tracking as a mode of generating self-knowledge or achieving goals of self-improvement, others are required to track themselves or are monitored in employment, social welfare or in education settings – sometimes with little opportunity to escape the gaze of others (Lupton, 2016). People are objectified, and their embodied labour exploited, through such technologies and systems as automated work environments (Delfanti, 2021).

Not all dataveillance is conducted for the purposes of exploitation, however. Recent discussions of the practices of using datafication and dataveillance for the care of other humans have noted the intimacy and relationality of such practices. This mode of dataveillance – sometimes referred to as 'careful' or 'caring dataveillance' – is conducted out of a sense of obligation and duty to people requiring care, such as infants and small children (Lupton, 2019a) or elderly relatives (Hjorth and Lupton, 2021). Nonetheless, as is the case with any relation of care, issues of control related to digitized practices of surveillance remain, as such practices may involve lack of consent on the part of those who are watched by carers with the use of monitoring devices (for example, in the case of infants and children or older people experiencing cognitive decline), as well as flouting vulnerable people's personal data privacy (Lupton and Williamson, 2017).

These issues concerning dataveillance have yet to be fully considered when animals are brought into the field of datafied watching. Orienting the analytical focus away from human-centric preoccupations draws attention to the ways that the interests and wellbeing of animals may be either promoted or undermined via the process of dataveillance. Such an approach should begin with a more-than-human perspective, acknowledging that the flourishing of animals and that of humans are connected and relational, situated within much broader networks of things at a global scale. We can begin to consider what it means for our relationships with animals when our knowledge of and relationships with the latter are increasingly datafied and digitized. How do dataveillance processes affect our practices and feelings towards animals? How do these practices contribute to or detract from our relational connections with animals?

Datafied wildlife

Digital devices have been suggested as a way of contributing streams of data that can allow continuous analysis of wild animals' bodily activities and functions for biological and ecological research purposes. As I noted in the Introduction chapter, the term 'Internet of Animals' has previously been used in relation to the ICARUS monitoring project involving IoT technologies and digital sensors to track wildlife remotely. An article published on *Nature*'s website (Curry, 2018) outlines the work of the scientist leading the ICARUS initiative, biologist Martin Wikelski. The article describes the Internet of Animals as involving dataveillance systems installed on satellites and space stations that allow for diverse sets of big data about animals to be connected and analysed: 'In the long run, Wikelski hopes the system will connect so many individuals – from elephants and warblers to baby sea turtles – that it could create an internet of animals. It could use the movements and habits of wild creatures to reveal patterns in much the same way that mobile-phone apps pinpoint traffic and illuminate people's social networks' (Curry, 2018).

Research initiatives by scientists such as those involved in ICARUS are clearly ground-breaking, expensive and highly technical advances in animal monitoring. The excerpt from the *Nature* article emphasizes the connection of animals to each other, but this 'connection' is remotely achieved by joining up data sets about them to establish 'patterns' of behaviour. It is notable that an analogy is made by the author to the ways that information about people's movements and social networks can be collected and analysed using far more everyday technologies: apps on their phones.

As is the case for other IoT applications, these 'smart' forms of animal dataveillance are promoted as offering the benefits of continuous automation of the collection of data and data-driven decision-making. The level of detail and intimacy achieved by continual digital tracking has been incorporated into animal protection and conservation efforts. In chapter 2, I described some volunteer animal enthusiast and citizen science initiatives that have used crowdsourcing to gather digital data about wildlife. In other initiatives conducted by scientists, ecologists and conservation managers, wearable devices and RFID (Radio Frequency Identification) chips are placed on wild animals' bodies. Drones are used to monitor wild animal species as part of restoration ecology efforts, and deployed for geolocating, counting and identifying wildlife, mapping habitats and breeding grounds, and managing wildfires (Robinson et al., 2022). Scientists are also experimenting with facial recognition technologies to identify wildlife such as seals using a database of photos previously taken of the creatures' faces, as a less invasive way of tracking their movements and habits (Mowbray, 2022). Wildlife cartographies can be easily generated with the digital data from these monitoring systems, ready to be used in conservation initiatives (Adams, 2017).

In some cases, dataveillance technologies have been used as a way of protecting wild animals from harm. Other initiatives include the BirdVision project, which equips windmills with digital sensors that can recognize when birds are flying nearby, slowing down or stopping the rotation of the windmills' blades when the birds come close enough to be harmed (Bossert and Hagendorff, 2021). Some digital conservation initiatives rely predominantly on generating aural data as a form of monitoring ecosystems. The Elephant Listening project protects elephants against poaching by informing rangers about the elephants' location and monitoring for sounds such as gunfire emitted from poachers' weapons (Bossert and Hagendorff, 2021). The Rainforest Connection project (2022) involves the building and deployment of open acoustic monitoring systems used to halt illegal logging and poaching activities in rainforests in over twenty countries, and also enables biodiversity measurement and monitoring. Solar-powered acoustic streaming devices are placed high in tree-top canopies, continuously recording soundscapes of the area. These aural data are analysed using machine learning to identify sounds of chainsaw activity and animal calls, indicating which species are active, and their numbers. The data are shared with local rangers so that they can take timely action. An app is also offered to people who want to listen to the sounds of a rainforest in real time.

Some researchers adopting a One Health perspective have advocated for the use of biosensors for monitoring animals' health as a form of sentinel tracking for the impact of environmental degradation and contamination, and of the emergence of new infectious diseases on the humans who share the same ecosystem (Frazzoli et al., 2022). In such dataveillance initiatives, digital sensors are placed on insects in efforts to generate useful data to contribute to environmental protection and sustainability. Honeybees are commonly monitored in this way, due to the vital role they play in pollination for both wild and domesticated plant species and in the production of honey as a commercial product. One initiative – dubbed 'Big brother for bees' by the researchers – experimented with deploying wireless sensor network systems to monitor bee colonies, with digital infrared cameras, microphones and thermal imaging technologies to collect image and audio data. These data enable beekeepers to gain a comprehensive view of in-hive conditions as well as helping them monitor the movements of the bees when they are flying outside the hives (Murphy et al., 2015). A similar project, referring to the 'smart beehive', deployed in-hive sensors to track levels of CO_2, O_2, pollutant gases, temperature and relative humidity, together with weather data (sunshine, rain and temperature). Algorithmic analysis of the digital data generated from this system was applied to discern relationships between the beehive information and meteorological conditions. The researchers claimed that this 'smart beehive' could contribute to short-term weather forecasting efforts, together with climate change monitoring (Edwards-Murphy et al., 2016).

Other projects have deployed wearable sensors fitted onto bees' bodies to track their movements. University of Washington researchers (Iyer et al., 2019) have developed what they call 'a flying wireless platform', including sensors, location-tracking receivers, data storage and a rechargeable battery, that has been attached to bumblebees as a 'backpack' unit. The sensors, which weigh the equivalent of seven grains of uncooked rice, measure the bees' location and movements together with environmental temperature, light intensity and humidity levels. According to the researchers, 'the bees can collect data for hours', while agricultural or climate monitoring drones need recharging after only 10 or 20 minutes. Once the bees are back in the hive, the battery they carry is recharged by an in-hive charging unit. Such efforts, described as the 'Internet of biological things' or the 'Living IoT', bring together what might be called 'insect intelligence' with 'smart' technologies. They are described as 'biology-based solutions' to create 'a mobile IoT platform'. As researchers argue: 'Such an approach takes advantage of these tiny, highly efficient biological insects which are ubiquitous in many outdoor ecosystems, to essentially provide mobility for free' (Iyer, 2022).

In some situations, digital devices are used to monitor animals that are considered to be pests, as a way of managing them – in some cases, involving culling them. In Europe, wild boars and their feeding sites are tracked by infrared and CCTV cameras, with the data generated by these technologies used by hunters and farmers to kill or control the movements of these animals. Drones are also used in boar hunts. Plans are underway to fit some boars with wearable devices to identify their geolocation and movements (von Essen et al., 2021). In Australia, the ToadScan platform and phone app, supported by the Australian government, a research centre, industry bodies and a charitable foundation, assist people in recording the presence of cane toads (an introduced species that has proliferated in north-eastern Australia, causing damage to crops and wildlife) in their area. Users who download the app are provided with instructions on how to identify a cane toad and record sightings of the toads or their tadpoles and eggs, and also the call of the toad, to generate a 'toad map' of their area. Participants are also encouraged to take photos of damage to the environment caused by cane toads and record evidence of toad control activities which they engage in or come across (ToadScan, 2022).

While these approaches recognize the intertwining of animal and human health together with that of other elements of ecosystems, they tend to privilege human health over that of other creatures and other dimensions of the environment. Animals are either positioned as a risk to humans (for example, by acting as reservoirs or vectors of infection or as pests requiring culling) or as proxies for ecological health (digitized versions of canaries in coal mines). In the case of the 'Living IoT' initiative, bees are rendered into digital-insect vehicles for environmental monitoring purposes – further objectifying their bodies as tools for human use.

'Smart' agriculture

Sociotechnical imaginaries expressed in narratives referring to 'smart agriculture', 'smart farms', 'AgTech' or 'precision agriculture' rely on the power of terms such as 'smart' and 'precision' to position such technologies as forward-looking, innovative, accurate – and, above all, superior to older practices and technologies (Lupton, 2020b). Particularly in industry-focused documents, such as developer websites, there is constant reference to the benefits promised by smart agriculture initiatives – including improved crop yield, saving workers' time and optimal animal husbandry, leading to increased productivity and profits for farmers. Robotic and other automated systems are presented as ways to perform repetitive tasks faster and more efficiently and precisely (Lockie et al., 2020). Terms such as 'AI', 'automation' and 'machine learning' are employed to promise data-driven decision support for farmers, who are presumed to be able to drill down into these data streams to acquire better knowledge of their animals (Karthick et al., 2020; Niloofar et al., 2021).

The concept of the 'digital twin' is also employed in new initiatives involving model simulation to contribute to animal management. The digital twin metaphor, first emerging in industry use contexts, describes the idea that data modelling, data visualization and machine learning software can be used to configure a detailed digital simulation. This simulation is then used to help understand and predict the ways that various elements in a complex system interact. Digital twins digitally model animals' bodies, using the big data generated from monitoring technologies together with other data sets, such as those derived from environment and climate monitoring, genetic analysis and animal health information. The intention is to use automated decision-making to understand better how to promote the health, feeding and reproduction parameters of animals so as to develop 'healthy growing conditions' as well as indicators of animal wellbeing such as early disease detection (Mokal and Sharma, 2020). Broadening out this concept, initiatives such as the 'Digital Future Farm' project in the Netherlands involve digital twin modelling of farm environments, including data sets on animals from a range of sources, together with biological data about the soil, grass and crop growth, fertilizer use and climate conditions of the land on which the animals live (Athanasiadis, 2022).

In an IoT deployment involving technologies that are highly interventionist, 'virtual fencing' systems are currently used in some locations for animal husbandry. These systems involve the use of sensory cues provided by digital technologies to encourage grazing animals such as cattle and sheep to keep within defined boundaries without the need for physical barriers. In some cases, this approach is used to protect environmentally sensitive areas from damage wrought by the animals, to assist with rewilding and conservation efforts (Campbell et al., 2020). The animals are fitted with a collar with a sensor that emits a warning sound when they stray too close to the digitized boundary. If they continue, a low-level electric shock is administered via the collar in the attempt to train them to understand that they should not be in that area (Lee et al., 2018).

In some instances, datafication of animals has been incorporated into First Nations' husbandry practices. Indigenous Sámi communities living in northern Sweden use collars fitted with GPS transmitters to monitor the reindeer they herd. The data generated by these devices help these herders in their animal husbandry by allowing them to 'get to know' the reindeer and their habits. Traditional Sámi knowledge of reindeer developed over generations of observing their movements and grazing practices is augmented with these locative data. Given that the reindeer range over wide terrains, often out of sight of the herders and in the dark or extreme weather conditions, the dataveillance practices allow for much greater visibility of their movements, helping the herders to plan their own daily activities and travel. There are additional environmental benefits, as herders can better manage their use of vehicles. The herders interpret the data together with their long-held knowledge of the animals' behaviour and the geographical and climate conditions in and through which the reindeer move (Kuoljok, 2019).

Farmed sea creatures are also monitored with digital tracking devices to contribute to productivity and save time for farmers. For example, in the Australian state of Tasmania, farmers have fitted oysters with biosensors to determine how environmental conditions such as water temperature, water pressure, light levels and salinity affect their growth and health. The sensors, placed outside on the oyster shell, monitor the oysters' heartbeat, track whether the shell is open or closed to determine their feeding habits, and record the depth of the water in which the oysters have settled. These data can be analysed in real time as a way of keeping track of the oysters' biometric indicators and determining how to produce the 'best oyster' for the human oyster consumption market. The expectation is that oyster farmers using this system will save time by not having to take oysters out of the baskets in which they live to see how much they have grown and whether they are ready for harvesting (Rutkin, 2014).

With an increasing emphasis on farm animal welfare, dataveillance technologies are used in some places to ensure that the health and wellbeing of animals are supported. Legal scholars interested in animal welfare (Manning et al., 2021) have suggested that deploying wearable devices (or 'on-animal' devices, as they describe these technologies) may be a way to assess whether farm animals are treated well by farmers and thereby assist with their compliance with or legal enforcement of animal welfare legislation. Technologies that are sometimes referred to as 'The Internet of Things in Animal Healthcare' (Karthick et al., 2020) are currently in development, used to collect data on animals' bodily functions and health states. Biosensors, wearable devices and software similar to those employed for human healthcare are attached to animals' bodies, tracking vital signs such as their body temperature, heart rate, blood pressure, physical activity and respiratory rate. Animals have been fitted with tiny sensor devices with GPS and RFID tags that monitor their movements and spatial location on farming properties: particularly useful for farmers with very large land use. Drones and other mobile surveillance cameras can be implemented to take images of animals to monitor them for signs of distress. Recording movement, standing and grazing patterns using digital devices such as drones have been promoted as helping farmers to become aware of the possibility of illness or injury in their animals and to take action early (Lockie et al., 2020).

So-called robotic or automatic milking technologies are the latest in a long line of mechanized devices for extracting milk from cows. Developers of the more recent incarnation of these technologies are careful to highlight 'cow comfort' in their spiels for technologies that attach to the animals' bodies. Thus, for example, the Lely company's website claims that their Lely Astronaut technology is 'The new milestone in cow comfort' (Lely.com, 2022). According to the following text, 'The cow is central to all of the products that we develop.' The company asserts that their new designs result in 'the most natural way to milk' which promotes the cows' 'freedom to choose when to eat, drink, rest or be milked', which in turn promotes the 'comfort' and 'wellbeing' of the cows. The technologies that configure such a 'natural' milking experience for the cow are, somewhat paradoxically, highly interventionist. They feature a hybrid robotic arm and 'i-flow' technology which leads the cow into the milking apparatus with a clear pathway and the ability to see other cows in its environs, thus resulting in a 'stress free' and therefore 'productive' cow. The robotic arm is the device that extracts milk from the cows' udders, using a digitized 'teat detection system' that is promoted as fast and accurate, again reducing stress for the cow. Such rhetoric promotes the idea that the old way of milking – by humans, by hand, sitting close to the flanks of the cows and engaging in multisensory encounters with them (Holloway and Bear, 2017) – is somehow less 'natural'.

Researchers adopting a more-than-human perspective have examined the implications of these types of systems for how they have transformed the everyday lives of both the humans who manage and work on dairy farms and the cows who reside there. Lewis Holloway and Christopher Bear (2017) argue that the transition from hand-milking to automatic milking systems has affected these human–animal relationships. Different modes of cow and human agency are formed with and through these technologies. Farmers using such systems agreed that they allow the cows more 'freedom', as they go to be milked of their own volition, rather than adhering to the previous schedule set by the farmers and their workers. Yet dairy cows have very limited agency within the socio-spatial-technological contexts of the industrial dairy farm. Automated milking systems may offer them a small element of choice, but they cannot escape the regulated and surveillance apparatus, built for humans' needs and benefits, in which they have been bred and are maintained all their lives. The cows' flesh-and-blood bodies are still manipulated and positioned as, above all, machines for generating milk for the consumption and economic benefit of humans.

All milking systems, whether digitized or not, most likely involve pain and discomfort for dairy cows. When farmers who formerly hand-milked were once able to check the health and wellbeing of the cows every time they handled their bodies (looking for signs of infection in the teats, for example), automated systems remove this direct human–animal connection (Holloway and Bear, 2017). The cows' capacity for 'freedom' and 'agency', therefore, is viewed from a human perspective. While bovine and human agency are intertwined in these husbandry and milking systems, the human-centric values of economic productivity and efficiency are paramount. The individual needs and wellbeing of each cow are subsumed when milking systems become increasingly automated. As Holloway and Bear (2017: 216) assert, 'encountering and "using" the technologies change what it is to be human or bovine'. Indeed, as they point out, domesticated animals such as cows might be viewed as themselves human-made technologies, due to the long history of manipulation of their bodies through breeding strategies to render them more useful and productive for humans.

Pet tech

A plethora of mobile apps and digital tracking devices targeted at pet owners have been released in recent years. As is evident in human-focused efforts to monitor intimate human others, the values of better knowledge of pets' health and relational connections driven by data are expressed in discourses of pet tracking. The social imaginaries contributing to the developers' promotional discourses for such pet monitoring technologies are very similar to those articulated in discourses seeking to encourage humans to use self-tracking apps and devices.

Many of the more recent monitoring wearable devices track a multitude of aspects of pets' lives and movements, promoting the promise that data-driven decision-making will generate greater insights into these animals' health and wellbeing and assist with their care. MyPet can be used for tracking veterinary care, such as vaccinations and medication, and Dog Clicker Training to help owners reinforce positive behaviour in their dogs. The PetParent app helps owners to connect with others and find services in their local area for their pets, while the Rover app can be used to find a pet sitter or dog walker. Some devices operate as location trackers, letting owners know if their animal has strayed beyond a set 'safe zone'. The Wag app operates to help owners monitor their dogs when they are taken on walks by other people, including the dog's urination and defecation activities and their geolocation. Several digital tracking devices and apps are directly connected to veterinary expertise. For example, a main selling point of the Maven Smart Collar and app is that the data generated by the wearable can be used by the owner to conduct health checks, with vets available to provide advice via chat or video calls if any concerning notifications arise.

'Smart' leashes and dog harnesses are also available for dog owners who want to track their own and their dog's physical activity. The developers of Fitbark contend that, using their smart GPS-tracking wearable device, people can track their own physical activity and that of their dogs, improving health and fitness for both: 'You and your pup, healthy together'. Fitbark is also worn on the dog's collar and is 'human tracker friendly', so that the data generated by this wearable can be linked to a human-worn device. The promissory narrative advanced on the website is that owners can 'get motivated' and 'monitor progress together' with their dog. The Fitbark tracks a plethora of details about the dog's body: minute-by-minute physical activity, sleep quality, distance travelled, calories burned and anxiety levels. The website claims that dog owners will be able to detect health problems in their pets – such as skin conditions, stress or reduced mobility – early by continually checking these data, together with monitoring chronic conditions such as diabetes or arthritis. The dog's data sync with smartphone devices so that owners can receive real-time updates of the dog's health statistics, activity and geolocation (Fitbark.com, 2022). The ilume platform and app combine the affordances of online ordering of fresh dog food with personalized meal plans for the animals. The food's nutrient levels are algorithmically calculated from data generated from the dog's activity and sleep tracking app. The ilume website promotes an imaginary of 'mindful insights into your dog's daily life' contributing to 'optimised meal portions' (ilume.com, 2022).

Owners of both dogs and cats are targeted as potential consumers of home-based camera monitoring systems for watching pets as they move around the house. These devices are similar to baby monitors, offering movement sensors and image streams so that pet owners can keep an eye on the animals while they are out of the house. One example is the Ebo by the Enabot company, marketed as an 'AI family companion robot' (Enabot, 2022). These 'smart companions' are promoted as 'allow[ing] you to connect to your loved ones at all times' (including pets and family members) but also acting as security surveillance detectors that monitor 'every corner of your house' and let you know 'when suspicious activities have been detected'. Owners can watch the pet through an app streaming video on their phone, and can interact with it (a video on the Enabot website shows a woman greeting her cat with 'Hi cutie' by speaking into her phone).

Automated toys, self-cleaning litter trays (for example, the Litter-Robot device) and pet feeders, with dispensers for dry food and water fountains, are also available for cats and dogs. The iFetch dog toy is an automated dog ball launcher for inside or outside the home, designed to be interactive so that it responds to the dog's actions (Goifetch.com, 2022). The Skymee company (2022) has several automated devices designed for pet care and entertainment. The Dog Treat Dispenser is marketed as allowing owners to enjoy a remote 'happy catch game with your pet by tossing his favourite treats'. The Fury Bone Interactive Smart Pet Toy for dogs and cats is a 'smart bone' and offers both automated and manual control so that the animals can amuse themselves in the absence of their owner. Some devices provide a combination of features. The Owl Robot, with an owl-like face, has been designed to roll itself around on the floor, offering the capacities of pet entertainment, a surveillance camera streaming images of the pet to the owner's phone and a treat dispenser all in one. Infrared sensing is used in these robot toys to detect the animal's presence and respond to it. Petcube devices, made by a different company, offer camera surveillance with two-way audio, remote treat dispensing, an interactive laser toy and 24/7 online vet assistance, together with a pet insurance plan (Petcube.com, 2022).

Imaginaries that position these devices as communicative mediators between people and their pets are frequently expressed in websites marketing the technologies. These include the Whistle Health smart device, a wearable device placed on a dog's collar. According to the developer's website, Whistle Health represents 'the next generation of pet care', involving 'six years of research' and 'trillions of data points' to develop. In describing how the device works, it is claimed that: 'Every lick, scratch, and sip tells a story. Whistle smart devices are designed to reveal the full picture of your pet's health. They track and translate activity, behavior, location, wellness, and more. All so you can better understand their health and bring them personalized, proactive care.' Furthermore, the

Whistle Health company asserts that using this data-driven technology 'give[s] pets a voice', revealing 'all the things your pet can't tell you', and therefore operating as 'your own, personal pet translator' (Whistle.com, 2022).

Yet another imaginary suffuses the promotional discourses for the TailTalk tail sensor. Its developers, the DogStar company (DogStar, 2022), promote the device as 'the world's first dog emotion sensor' and argue that attaching their device to a dog's tail will help owners identify the animal's emotional state. The sole purpose of this wearable device, therefore, is to help dog owners interpret the signs and signals that the dog's movement of its tail is attempting to convey: such as which people, places or toys make the creature feel happy or stressed. According to the TailTalk website, the device 'reveals the peaks and valleys of your dog's happiness throughout the day' as the tail movement data are collected, processed and reported to an app on the owner's phone. The website proclaims that 'The tail is the dog's social interface, like a smile is for humans.' These narratives are underpinned by the assumption that humans cannot readily interpret with their own embodied senses what their pet's tail movements are communicating: they need a digital device and its algorithmic processing capacities to undertake this task. TailTalk is therefore marketed as a digital communicative device for translating an embodied form of communication.

Thus far, only a small number of academic studies have investigated how pet owners are using these technologies. A UK-based study of sixty-nine dog owners found that a quarter of the respondents said that they used digital technologies related to their pets – including training apps, surveillance cameras, activity or health trackers, smart toys and smart feeders (McParlan and van der Linden, 2021). Research into people's experiences of living with smart home technologies has sometimes surfaced unexpected uses of the technologies for caring for companion animals. For example, a study involving Australian families who were early adopters of smart home technologies showed that the participants often used these devices to engage in caring from remote locations by checking that their pets, and also their children or older family members, were safe and protected (Strengers et al., 2019a). In another project involving developing future-oriented scenarios about smart energy use systems, Strengers and colleagues (2019b) identified important factors such as people wanting to cater for the needs of their pets, keeping them warm and comfortable when they were home alone.

In her book on households' digital self-tracking during the COVID crisis, involving participants from Australia, Europe, Japan, New Zealand, the UK and the USA, Mariann Hardey (2022) had not specifically set out to investigate how pets were incorporated into these practices. Nonetheless, given that people were relying more on their intimate relationships with their pets for companionship during periods of lockdown and stay-at-home orders, Hardey found that self-tracking practices were naturally extended to these animals. Her participants gave examples of fitting their dogs or cats with activity monitors to supplement family members' fitness tracking efforts, and using phone apps to monitor aspects of their pets' behaviours, such as their eating and sleeping patterns. While they may initially have begun tracking their pets for fun or curiosity, these practices were strongly associated with people's concern about the health and wellbeing of their pets, contributing to their affective bonds in ways they considered positive and caring. Such digitized intimate forms of caring were very similar to the ways Hardey's participants discussed using tracking of other family members as part of close familial relationships.

In my online survey of people's use of digital technologies in relation to animals, 16 per cent of respondents reported using smartphone apps, wearable devices or any other 'smart' devices to better understand or care for their pet/s or for any other animals. These technologies were mostly used to check on pets in the home or monitor their health indicators:

> When I travelled (before COVID, hopefully after too), I would use a webcam with a connected app to check on my cats to make sure they were ok and their sitter was doing a good job – the sitter knew about the camera, of course.

> I used a cat diary to keep a track of my past cat's health issues: i.e. keeping track of weight.

> PetDesk is an app that can be used to book vet appointments. I use this to monitor milestone appointments for my puppy and to book check-ups with the vet. LAK Exclusive is an app used for booking pet care services through our dog trainer.

There are resonances in the findings of these studies with those exploring the motivations of parents to monitor digitally the bodies of their infants and small children (Lupton, 2019a; Lupton and Williamson, 2017), or adult children's practices in employing digital devices to track their ageing parents' health and wellbeing (Hjorth and Lupton, 2021). People's strong desire to connect with, feel close to and express love for their companion animals drives the use of these technologies. People's positioning of their pets as beloved members of their family who deserve intensive monitoring as part of caring is clearly evident in such accounts.

Dataveillance and human–animal relationships

There have been many insights offered in areas such as critical data studies and surveillance studies about the implications for humans of datafying and digitizing their bodies and environments (Lupton, 2016; Lupton and Williamson, 2017; Lyon, 2018; van Dijck, 2014). As these analyses have demonstrated, while these processes can offer people better understanding of their bodies and their selves, they are also reductionist and partial. Most of the complex affective and multisensory dimensions of human embodiment, selves and social relationships are ignored or simply cannot be captured by digitization and datafication (Lupton, 2015, 2016, 2019b; Lupton et al., 2022). There are related implications of these practices for how humans' knowledges and understandings of other animals contribute to the affective ties and relational connections they have with them. Sales pitches for animal monitoring devices rely heavily on the idea that datafied knowledge is superior to embodied knowledge. People are assumed to be less capable of detecting aspects of animals' bodies or behaviours – or, in some cases, less able to care properly for their animals – than automated technologies and data-driven software. There are implications of the expanding use and reliance upon these technologies for the future of humans' relationships with animals across species: including farmed animals, wild animals and pets.

The developers and other promoters of digital technologies for monitoring and measuring human bodies assert that digital data offer compelling and better knowledge and understanding that humans' flesh-and-blood sensing capacities are unable to generate or process (Lupton, 2016, 2019b; Lupton et al.,

2022). It is the deficiencies of human sentience and bodies, therefore, for which such technologies promise to compensate, rather than that of other animals. In particular, these datafied relationships rely on the sense of sight (viewing data visualizations about animals such as metrics, graphs or digital twin models) above all other sensory engagements. They close off the empathic connections and knowledges that humans can develop about animals when they can touch, smell or hear them, and encourage broad generalizations about animals' experiences and agencies, rather than treating them as individuals. As these technologies increasingly become automated and driven by algorithmic data processing, human interpretation, sensory judgement and decision-making expertise may be relegated to the margins as less accurate or more biased (Adams, 2017).

Jacqueline Bos and colleagues (2018) argue that the ethos and practices of digitized datafication applied to animals in smart farming systems operate to objectify animals as commercial commodities that are parts of the machinery and technologies of the datafying systems. While there may be some emphasis on gathering information to support animal welfare and environmental sustainability efforts in these data-driven systems, this purpose tends to be subordinate to commercial and economic productivity imperatives. In an industrial farming context which already has moved towards the objectification of animals as possessions for human exploitation (McCance, 2012; Taylor and Twine, 2014; Tester, 1991), this focus can disrupt what remains of traditional relationships of caring and empathy that exist between farmers and the animals they manage, detracting from the sensory knowledges and strong affective connections that accumulate when farmers have direct embodied contact with the animals. When care is digitized and datafied, it becomes remote: a matter of interpreting and applying data-driven decisions. Such processes detract from farmers' ability to sense the needs of the animals and thereby provide responsive care that can support the animals' quality of life, treating them as individuals with needs and rights rather than as things (Bos et al., 2018).

In chapter 2, I discussed the privacy implications of monitoring animals for political purposes or as part of citizen science initiatives. These incursions into animals' private lives include not only the visual media discussed earlier in that chapter – such as memes, GIFs and TikTok and YouTube videos – but also newer ways of digitizing animals, such as placing biosensors, RFID tags or tiny video cameras on animals' bodies or in their habitats for dataveillance purposes. Most analyses of digital data privacy concerning the datafication of animals focus on the implications for humans, should data about their animals – and, by extension, themselves – be exploited for commercial gain, leaked or hacked. A study of dog owners found that few had considered data security and privacy issues in relation to information about their pet. Those people who did so express concerns about their dog or other property being stolen should hackers gain access to data about their pet, or third parties profiting from the information (McParlan and van der Linden, 2021). So too, discussions of the potential harms of dataveillance operating in the context of farms tend to focus only on the humans that are part of these systems. For instance, a discussion of the 'surveillance farm' by surveillance studies scholar Francisco Klauser (2018) draws attention to the problems of vulnerability of the digital systems involved and ownership of the data. Klauser also highlights the power of the 'Big

Agriculture' actors who are part of the arrangements by which many smart farming technologies are developed, marketed and implemented. The participation of animals or other living things within these dataveillance governance technologies receives only a passing mention.

These kinds of case studies and examples provide intriguing insights into the mundane dimensions of 'smart' technologies as they are imbricated within animal–human–digital assemblages. These analyses highlight how humans' feelings and bodies are co-produced and entangled with animals through digitized systems, and draw attention to the emergent and dynamic more-than-digital dimensions of these more-than-human worlds. This is not to claim that technologies are necessarily or only harmful to humans or animals, but rather to point to the intersections and intra-actions of these human–animal assemblages and consider how relational connections and agential capacities may be opened or shut down when digital technologies are brought into human–animal relationships. Like the human 'quantified self' (Lupton, 2016, 2019b), the 'quantified animal' is a digitized and datafied sociotechnical being that is always only incomplete. While we may be able to ascertain some elements of other animals' experiences and sentience from the digital data or images that are captured from them using digital technologies, much more remain mysterious to us. Given that technologies to conduct dataveillance on animals are human-led, with human interests paramount, the quantified animal is a flesh–data assemblage that can be inferior to how we might learn about and engage with animals using the sensory and affective capacities of our own bodies. In the next chapter, the powerful affective forces generated by cuteness, celebrity and therapy cultures as they drive relational connections in human–animal relationships are identified and analysed for what they reveal about the onto-ethico-epistemological dimensions of these assemblages.

4
Animal Cuteness, Therapy and Celebrity Online

In the two previous chapters, I have discussed the affective forces and relational connections generated with and through digital media and devices, including the political and economic dimensions of humans' treatment of animals and the application of dataveillance technologies. The present chapter also focuses on affect, but with a greater emphasis on the depiction of animals as cute, amusing or therapeutic in digital media cultures. There is a particular focus on the ways that animals are used to communicate, embody or ameliorate human feelings, and to generate and share intimacy and conviviality among those who engage with these visualizations.

Catness and cuteness on social media

From the early days of the internet and the World Wide Web, domestic cats have been a dominant animal species in digital cultures. In 2008, Jody Berland reflected on the cultural dimensions of the digitized images of cats that had already been flooding the internet for some years, and the implications for human–feline relations. She noted that affective forces pervaded humans' reactions to these cat images – including as expressed by those people who are annoyed by the prevalence of these animals on the internet or find others' reactions overly sentimental or trivial. Berland argued that people's enchantment with these widely shared cat images sprang from the innocence, sweetness, soft tactility, self-possession and luxurious sensuality displayed by the cats. She suggested that, as part of the sharing economy, digitized images of cats contribute to convivial relationships between people, spreading positive affects between them.

Radha O'Meara's (2014) analysis of live action cat videos on YouTube identified similar features. As O'Meara argues, the popularity of these videos springs from the entertainment value of watching cats engage in surprising or amusing activities, as recorded by amateurs using their mobile devices and set in domestic environments. These typical features combine to present scenes of spontaneity, universality and intimacy. There is a surprise factor in many of the videos, related in most cases to cats engaging in activities that are unexpected or human-like, or which feature the animals doing something that is so typically 'cat-like' that it is worthy of note. Cats are often presented as 'simpletons' in reacting strongly to everyday items or practices that people find mundane. The spectacle of the video – and the strong affective force that draws viewers in – is mostly generated by these elements of surprise: the cat shown initially as calm but then reacting strongly to a thing or action staged by the human. As a genre, such cat videos tend to represent domestic felines as sharing common qualities of 'catness' – all of which humans find attractive, dramatic or appealing in some way. O'Meara argues that human viewers enjoy the spectacle of 'natural' and unselfconscious animal behaviour that is documented in these videos.

_____

Cats – and especially kittens – are also typically figured as 'cute' in digital cultures and sharing economies. 'I Can Haz CheezBurger?' (2022a) is one section of an internet content aggregator platform CheezBurger, founded by a Seattle-based company in 2007 and still highly popular. It features a diverse array of animal videos, GIFs, memes and photos, derived from across the internet. While the CheezBurger site advertises its content as helping to 'find all your funny in one place', not all of its animal content is amusing: appealing pets and adorable infant animals are in abundance. Cats predominate, but dogs also feature, together with some other animals such as rabbits, guinea pigs, bears and baby animals of many species. There are the 'Top 20 cat memes of the week', 'Meet the newly adopted [pet] faces of the week', reactions to pet images from Reddit, collections of videos and memes from social media and content curation sites such as Pinterest under topics such as '20 cutest kittens of the week', and compilations of the latest popular TikTok videos featuring pets.

Reddit has played a central role in establishing the online cute economy (Meese, 2014). The sub-Reddit r/aww, created in January 2008, is still going strong, with over 30 million members. The 'About community' details describe the group as designed for 'Things that make you go AWW! Like puppies, bunnies, babies, and so on . . . A place for really cute pictures and videos!'. Even though there is mention of babies in the description, the Reddit topic is designated 'Animals and Pets', and images of animals predominate over infant humans. Dogs and cats are the most featured animals, while wild animals such as otters, possums and pandas are also favoured, with the occasional farm animal (particularly calves and lambs). Animals showing affection to each other (parents with their infants, members of different species playing, sleeping or cuddling together) are also popular on this forum.

The online cute economy typically features anthropomorphic portrayals of pets as 'fur babies' and their owners as 'pet parents'. Breeds of dogs and cats are frequently the topic of online discussion forums or Facebook groups. The Bulldog Lovers & Owners Facebook group, as one example, boasts 31,000 members. There are more specific groups for such topics as dogs with challenging behaviours (Reactive Dog Support Group, 26,000 members), and much broader groups such as Dog Lovers (more than 250,000 members – its tagline is 'We love Dogs. We love Animals. We love Peace. We love you all. No nudes – no sales'). Typical posts on the latter site include photographs of other members' dogs, which are duly responded to by other users with comments such as 'absolutely adorable' and 'beautiful baby'. Other common posts include announcements of a newly acquired dog (often referred to as 'my new fur baby'), dogs' birthday announcements ('Happy birthday – we love you!'), requests for advice concerning what to do if a dog has behavioural or health problems, and notifications of a dog's death (often euphemistically referred to as 'crossing the rainbow bridge'), accompanied by photos of the dog while it was alive and comments from users offering their heart-felt condolences.

Dogspotting is an extremely popular Facebook dog group, boasting almost 2 million members. This group combines dog enthusiasm with a 'dog spotting' game approach, offering canine-related entertainment as its predominant feature. Members post photos they have taken of random dogs they have encountered while going about their everyday activities. The rules stipulate that no one is allowed to post images of their own dogs, or dogs they have met before. Other members are invited to comment, respond with the Facebook array of emojis and bestow 'awards' for the best images. Here again, there are many references to 'fur babies' and 'dog parents' in the posts and comments. The images that tend to attract the most 'awards' show dogs that look extremely fluffy (often described as 'muppets'), those striking appealing poses (such as holding a human's hand or seemingly listening closely to a human playing an instrument or singing) and dogs wearing outlandish outfits or with highly manipulated fur colouring or trimming (for example, dogs with dyed fur). Puppies also score very well, due to being viewed as 'a cutie', 'cuddly', 'precious' or 'a sweetie'.

Instagram and Twitter are other popular sites for dog and cat lovers. The Twitter account 'Thoughts of a Dog' has more than 3.5 million followers. As the account title suggests, the anonymous content creator regularly tweets as if from the perspective of a golden Labrador (the account image shows this type of dog holding a large slice of watermelon in its mouth). The content is highly affect-driven, with the 'dog' tweeting such comments to followers as 'gooooob morning' and 'in case you forgot, I love you' with artfully imprecise spelling and punctuation.

A study conducted by animal–computer researchers (Aspling et al., 2018) analysed Instagram and Facebook posts by dog owners writing about their pets from the dog's perspective to determine to what extent these posts demonstrate understanding of and empathy with the dogs' lifeworlds. Aspling and colleagues argue that posting content about a dog on social media from its perspective can be a way of engaging imaginatively and empathetically with the dog, allowing dog owners to reflect on their relationships with their animals. They note the highly anthropomorphic aspects of this content, and that pet owners are typically referred to as 'mum' or 'dad'. In another project, media studies researcher Jessica Maddox (2021) conducted interviews with 23 people (mostly from the US but also a small number from the UK and Australia) who ran Instagram accounts on behalf of their pets. The interviews found that, for these people, portraying their pet on Instagram was a self-representational strategy, designed to position themselves in the role of pet lover. These amateur pet Instagrammers positioned their pets as beloved family members who required much love and attention, and were proud to share images of them on their Instagram accounts.

In my survey about people's use of digital media and devices related to animals, participants also made frequent reference to their pets as 'family'. They described how they used social media posts about their pets to forge connections with their family members, friends or others in their social networks.

> My dog has an Insta account, I use it to post pics about his life. His breeder follows it, as well as many of my friends. On my personal Insta account I post pics and video about my horse, as she is a big part of my life.

> I share pictures, videos and updates on my cats on Facebook, Instagram and Twitter. A lot of my friends/family are cat lovers, and generally seem to enjoy updates on what our cats are doing (and I similarly enjoy posts about other people's pets).

As was the case with people's use of digital tracking apps and devices for their pets (chapter 3), there are similarities here to how people portray human members of their family – and particularly infants and young children – in their social media accounts, or engage with others' content about young family members. Just as people often create digital profiles for their children, emphasizing their 'cuteness' or amusing qualities, as a way of expressing their love, pride, care and relational connections (Lupton, 2019a) to their offspring, so too these 'fur babies' are extensions of their owners' identities and intimate relational networks. There is a strong ethos of reciprocity and intimacy in this sharing economy: pet owners both enjoy sharing images and viewing other pet owners' content as part of a community of pet lovers.

Animals and digital celebrity cultures

The 'Grumpy Cat' phenomenon is one of the earliest and best-known examples of an animal internet celebrity. The feline bestowed with the moniker 'Grumpy Cat' (real name Tardar Sauce) possessed a facial appearance – particularly a downturned mouth – that made her look as if she was extremely cross (at least as humans interpret such a facial expression). This apparent grumpy face was the result of a facial disfiguration, caused by a dental underbite and feline dwarfism (Conard, 2021). From the first Grumpy Cat meme published to the internet in 2012, this animal has featured in countless memes concerning this feeling of annoyance or unhappiness. Indeed, the Grumpy Cat meme is often described as the beginning of mass collaborative meme culture. The brother of the cat's owner uploaded a photo of Tardar Sauce to the online discussion forum Reddit. The cat with the disconsolate expression very quickly captured the online popular imagination. According to the Know Your Meme website (an authority on all things meme-related), Reddit users soon began to digitally manipulate images taken from the original photo, adding captions to the image macro and sharing these images as memes. These memes reached the front page of Reddit within 24 hours, due to their popularity. Many of these memes included captions describing life from the cat's point of view: for example, 'I had fun once. It was awful' and 'Just put me down' (Know Your Meme, 2022). Within two days, the image had been viewed over a million times. Aware of the interest in the image, and wanting to prove that the photo was of a real cat's face and not photoshopped, the owner and her brother then made a 10-second video featuring the cat and uploaded it to YouTube (Conard, 2021). The video was entitled 'Do not disturb Grumpy Cat'. They later added more videos to the 'Real Grumpy Cat' channel, together accumulating tens of millions of views.

The cat Lil BUB was another feline with an unusual facial expression that received major attention on the internet. Like Grumpy Cat, Lil BUB's face was caused by multiple genetic abnormalities (Laforteza, 2014). Lil BUB's unusual appearance and small physique attracted a lot of attention on the internet after her owner created a Tumblr blog featuring images of her in 2011. Again, Reddit played a major role in amplifying Lil BUB's internet presence. She was used to promote the cause of cats with special needs, requiring higher levels of healthcare and attention from the humans caring for them. According to the website devoted to Lil BUB (lil bub.com, 2022), 'BUB was a very special, one of a kind critter', who was 'the runt of a healthy feral litter' found in a tool shed in rural Indiana, USA, in 2011. Although the cat was born with disabilities that left her with an undeveloped jaw, no teeth, a tongue that protruded, bulbous eyes and dwarfism, she lived until 2019, after receiving special care. The website goes on to claim that: 'In her life on Earth, BUB overcame great health challenges and celebrated many accomplishments before leaving our planet.' It seems that among her accomplishments was the spawning of a profitable retail line. The 'BUB store' on the website features a huge range of branded merchandise: phone grips, plush toys, coffee beans, commemorative books and coins together with the usual T-shirts, stickers, mugs, socks and calendars (and, more recently, face masks for COVID protection).

Grumpy Cat's fame reached such heights that she attended the SXSW Film Festival (an annual event held in Austin, Texas, celebrating the convergence of creative, tech and education cultures), a wax statue of her appeared at Madame Tussaud's, and a Lifetime film, 'Grumpy Cat's Worst Christmas Ever', was made with her in the lead role (Conard, 2021). In 2013, a multimedia art exhibition in Huntsville, Alabama, USA, was themed around Grumpy Cat, including artworks made with stained glass, paper, soap and chain mail, and the more traditional media of paintings and sculptures. Many types of clothing, stuffed toys, costumes, books, calendars, a series of comics and home wares have featured the cat's image (Know Your Meme, 2022). At the time of her death in 2019, Grumpy Cat's social media accounts had reached impressive follower numbers: 2.4 million on Instagram and 1.4 million on Twitter. Her demise was reported in major global news outlets, including the BBC, CNN and the *New York Times*. Twitter users using the hashtag #TweetAGrumpyFaceForGrumpy posted images of their own cats as a homage (Conard, 2021; Know Your Meme, 2022).

According to BuzzBingo (2022), Jiff Pom, a tiny Pomeranian dog who is known for his cuteness, is currently the most popular animal on TikTok, with a total of 517 million likes on that platform. The TikTok videos show Jiff Pom dressed in outfits, performing tricks such as waving, drinking water from a plastic cup at a cafe, sleeping cuddled up in a blanket, riding a skateboard, eating ice-cream, playing with toys and various other everyday activities in which children engage. Another, perhaps more surprising, entry in the popular TikTok animals list is the @floofnoodles account, which features ferrets that are manipulated to look as if they are cooking (with chefs' hats on) and looking forward to consuming the human dishes they have supposedly prepared (tongues out as if hungry to eat the food) – or dancing, dressed up in costumes to resemble human characters such as those from Harry Potter or popular singers such as Billie Eilish.

The most followed pet accounts on Instagram as of June 2020 were headed by Jiff Pom, well above the second listed animal Nala Cat, then Doug the Pug, Juniper & Friends, Grumpy Cat, Shinjiro Ono, Lil BUB, Tuna (breed: chiweenie), Venus the Two Face Cat and Loki the Wolfdog (Statista, 2020). Such 'animal influencers' have distinctive appearances or back stories that their owners draw on to receive and maintain social media users' interest. Like human influencers who have gained a huge following on social media platforms, many of the account owners have successfully monetized their 'brands'. Nala Cat was a stray cat who was adopted from an animal shelter. A Siamese/tabby mix, she has blue, slightly crossed eyes from her Siamese genes, together with the striping, rounded eyes and body shape of a tabby cat. According to her Instagram details, Nala Cat has received a Guinness World Record for 'the most famous cat' on that platform, based on 2020 metrics. Her Instagram and other social media accounts promote a cat food brand and the video game Farmville 3.

Not only can individual animals become very well known on social media and in GIFs and memes – thereby claiming status as 'animal online celebrities' or 'animal influencers' – but well-known animals can also be used together with human celebrities, characters or influencers. Sometimes well-known people have been presented alongside cat or dog images in social media sites or blogs that seek to convey the assumed personality or appearance of the human in the expression or appearance of the animal. In one example – and somewhat stretching the term 'celebrity' to include despotic leaders as well as actors, artists and musicians – a blog post on the site Bored Panda (Gabulaitė, 2016) presented no fewer than seventy-one comparison images of 'celebrity doppelganger animals'. Animals in these images were presented side-by-side with a photo of the human they purportedly resembled. The comparisons ranged from dogs looking like Vladimir Putin, Snoop Dog, Vladimir Lenin, Harrison Ford and John Travolta to cats supposedly resembling Leo DiCaprio, Adolf Hitler and Salvador Dali, a frog in a pose similar to one struck by Madonna, a whale compared with a pregnant Kim Kardashian, a giraffe positioned next to an image of Miley Cyrus and a caterpillar with shape and colouring similar to Donald Trump's hairstyle.

The urge towards anthropomorphism is clearly evident in these portrayals – but so too, there is a parallel zoomorphism of humans' appearances or personalities. Such depictions imply that audiences can better understand or categorize other people by positioning them as types of animals or as specific animals, drawing on their assumptions concerning what animals' bodily forms or facial expressions are revealing about their affective state or character. The politics of this type of digital media portrayal are intriguing to ponder. It may well be harmless fun when powerful white male celebrities are compared with animals, but what are the implications of using animal images to represent groups of people, such as women or people of colour, who have historically suffered or continue to be demeaned by their cultural positioning as animal-like (chapter 1)? Further, when images of controversial world figures such as Putin, Lenin or Hitler are juxtaposed with animals resembling them in some way, the effect is jarring, as it seems to both humanize and trivialize them, in a kind of warped 'cuteness' effect.

Animals as therapy in digital cultures

When the death of the YouTube star Mishka the Talking Husky was announced in 2017, comments on her YouTube channel by her fans and followers made frequent reference to how her videos (in which she was purportedly 'talking', due to subtitles provided by her owners to 'interpret' her vocalizations) had made them feel happy, joy, delight, and encouraged them to smile. People commented that the videos gave them a 'pick-me-up' when they were having a bad day and that they felt part of the dog's family and were grieving as if Mishka were their own pet.

It has long been noted that internet users viewing images of animals coded as cute or funny frequently express how important such viewing has been to helping them lift their low mood or cope with difficult situations or feelings. Many social media users will be familiar with the request of other users to flood their feed/timelines with 'cute' or 'funny' animals because that person is having a difficult time and needs cheering up. Users of such platforms as Twitter, TikTok, Reddit and Facebook often describe the practice of posting images of appealing animals as a 'timeline cleanser' – that is, providing anodyne or cheering content as a contrast and salve to the often dismaying, frightening or vituperative material that appears on these platforms. Indeed, Reddit hosts a highly popular subreddit, r/Eyebleach, which is specifically dedicated to such therapeutic contents. Members are required to post only 'nice' content (one of its rules is 'no sad content'): cute or amusing animal images feature strongly. Lists of animal memes, GIFs or videos are frequently headed with such medicalized titles as 'The weekly dose of cute cats', advertised as offering 'wholesomeness and pawsitivity and nothing but good vibes' (I Can Haz Cheezburger?, 2022b).

During the first two years of the COVID crisis, animals were strongly represented in digital visual media sought by people wanting distraction, the alleviation of boredom or loneliness, and a way of connecting to 'nature' while they were isolated inside their homes (Lupton, 2022). These relations were established or maintained via digital devices and platforms, with the use of memes, TikTok or YouTube videos, Facebook and Instagram posts featuring animals, and livestreaming services offering continuous feeds of animals going about their everyday lives. According to an article on 'the best animal live cams to watch to see animal babies this spring' published in mid-2021 (Weingarten, 2021), taking time out from tedious activities such as working from home or supervising children could be both an escape from the confines of the home and educational: a way to learn about nature. The article lists services such as shelters for puppies and kittens ('puppy cam' and 'kitten cam'), together with several options for watching livestreaming of lions, pandas, penguins, jellyfish, sharks, otters, puffins, sloths, elephants and tigers at zoos and aquariums around the world, baby animals on farms, and wild birds such as eagles and ospreys with cameras trained on their nests.

Social media users frequently upload, seek out or share appealing or amusing animal content in a deliberate effort to lighten their own and other users' moods or alleviate distress. People who were interviewed by Jessica Maddox about their practice of posting images of their pets to Instagram said that their primary motivation was to provide and spread joy to other Instagram users. They positioned their social media content as countering what they saw as the tendencies towards the portrayal of 'doom and gloom and capitalism' (Maddox, 2021: 3342) on the internet, or the often toxic exchanges on social media platforms that were harmful and detrimental to users' mood. The interviewees in Maddox's study referred to the role played by their pets' images in bringing moments of lightness, purity and happiness to Instagram, distracting them from the other disturbing and catastrophic news that is found on other sites. The interviewees also referred to following similar 'cute animals' accounts on Instagram and other social media so that they themselves could benefit from 'a burst of positivity in my Feed as I'm scrolling', as one person put it (Maddox, 2021: 3342), or the 'warm fuzzy feelings' that another participant said she felt when viewing other people's pets on social media (Maddox, 2021: 3343).

In my study, participants also often commented that they enjoyed and actively sought out viewing 'cute' or 'funny' animal content online as a form of therapy or stress relief. Similar to Maddox's Instagram users, their comments about these practices typically made reference to the endearing and entertaining qualities of the animals they found online – their 'goofiness' or 'cuteness' – and how these images can create positive affects in times that may be particularly difficult:

I follow some Instagram accounts featuring pet content, and also watch YouTube videos in my free time about pets/animals. I consider this a stress-relief practice.

On TikTok my 'for you page' has a lot of animal related things ranging from funny videos, animal care and simply just cute animals. I find it very entertaining and [it] makes me feel warm and fuzzy.

Many respondents also reported that they uploaded and shared content about their own pets or other animals to social media sites or using messaging apps, to entertain or raise the spirits of other users:

I upload pictures of my pets and occasionally funny animal images – e.g. goats near my home doing funny things or once when I had a peacock in my garden. I do this because animals are endearing and generate good feelings in others.

I often look at funny animal memes in order to share them with friends that I know will enjoy them.

My survey was conducted a year after the COVID-19 pandemic had been declared. Several people made direct reference to the difficult conditions of lockdowns and other experiences of isolation from others due to COVID restrictions, and how they posted animal content or engaged with others' posts as a way of coping:

I send pictures of my dog to friends – both individually and in private, closed groups – via messaging apps (WhatsApp, Signal) – and I post pictures of my dog to Twitter. I do this because my dog is adorable, my friends and I share pictures of our pets with each other all the time, and pets are a welcome distraction at the moment during the COVID-19 pandemic.

There were also comments about how uplifting or entertaining animal content provided a respite from the other online content people were viewing, which was described as too serious or confronting:

> Doggo memes – I am tagged in these a lot and particularly like the poems people write for animals! They are cute and it's a bit of a stress reliever to look at animal pictures that aren't related to animal abuse for a change.

> My children enjoy these videos and I think they are great because they keep them away from all the nasty things they might be exposed to on the internet. Here I am referring to funny cat videos and funny pet videos. I find these on my social media accounts like Instagram or YouTube and I watch these funny videos with my kids.

These comments show that animals are treated as therapeutic objects for improving people's mental health and general 'wellness' in digital cultures, and that people also engage in reciprocal practices of sharing animal visual media to support each other. These practices are undertaken to strengthen relational connections in people's social networks and to demonstrate and actively engage in care for other people in the attempt to improve their wellbeing.

The dark side of online cuteness and celebrity

Just as there is a longstanding tradition of according certain animals celebrity status in popular media, so too there is an accompanying tradition of the abuse and mistreatment of animals in the television and film industries: both documentary and fictional media (Malamud, 2012). There are few benefits of celebrity for animals, and many potential harms: including the extreme forms of objectification of the animals as spectacles and commodities for their owners or handlers. There are strong resonances of these depictions across all mainstream visual cultures. Mills (2017) describes the phenomenon of representing 'animals as dumb' in television cultures: lacking both an agential voice and (human-like) intelligence.

This exertion of the human gaze on the objectified animal perhaps reaches its apotheosis in the use of animals as fetishized sexual objects in pornography. But as Malamud (2012: 27) makes clear in his critique: 'The visual acculturation of animals is compelling to the human viewer, and the corollary cost to animals is the erasure of their actual being. Visual culture hegemonically monopolizes our modes of perception with regard to other species.' In these examples of animals featuring in visual culture, the individual needs of the animals become subsumed to humans' desire for how they want animals to behave for entertainment, scientific experimentation or amusement (Malamud, 2012) – and, increasingly, as objects of stress relief for humans' therapeutic purposes. Malamud (2012) interprets such uses of animals in visual culture as humans' will to exert control over their environments, which involves stripping animals of their dignity, self-determination and bodily control. Animals become props for human commodification, both highly visible as spectacles and invisible (because they are depersonalized).

Cuteness and animal celebrity cultures are integral to these contemporary forms of objectification and commodification. Adopting a Marxian critique, Allison Page (2016) argues that cute animal images have been used not only for content creators to monetize but also in the interests of the capitalist economic system as a way to motivate workers and distract them from the conditions of their lives. She sees cute animal videos as being used as a tool for coping with the drudgery of work and office life and the ill effects of the productivist ethos characterized in neoliberalist capitalism. According to Page, cuteness is central to strategies of self-care and top-down management of affect in the workplace. Images of adorable animals online are frequently accompanied by rhetoric that emphasizes the values of hard work and keeping focused and productive, even when times are tough. Many such images in fact show the animals sitting at desks and computers as if they are in the world of human work, dealing with the same time pressures and stresses. The makers of these videos attempt to depict crises as mundane, thereby reducing the affective harms of neoliberalism.

This analysis underscores that the trivializing of the banal comfort offered to millions of internet users by cute animal media fails to recognize the harder-edged dimensions of how these affects can be exploited to suit the capitalist ethos and the ever intensifying commodification of everyday life. Cuteness serves to provide 'our salve or reward' for the drudgery and pressures of life. Viewer and popular media commentary frequently positions these images as 'powerful vehicles through which humanity is revived, consoled, and/or healed from the suffering of the day' (Page, 2016: 79).

Other scholars have drawn attention to the power differential that is essential to the cuteness affect. Relations of care can be fraught with competing affects and struggles for control (Tronto, 1993): so, too, cuteness feelings can be ambivalent. Those who bestow the title of cuteness or are emotionally affected by cuteness are depicting the target of their affect as vulnerable, helpless and in need of protection (May, 2019). These observations can link to a wider discussion of the power relations involved in care. If the care or protective affective response is a vital force in the cuteness relationship, then close examination of these relations of care is also warranted (Parkinson, 2019). Cuteness is a relational force, just as any affective response involves relationality and intra-actions. It involves no little hint of patriarchal indulgence and infantilization, which can be used to put people (or animals) in their place as lesser beings. The desire to protect and care for a cute object is often entangled with feelings of mastery and control, or sometimes loss of control: feelings about cuteness can be experienced as overwhelming. It is notable that a typical response to cute animal images on the internet is to express feelings that are so extreme they seem to be physically violent: 'I am dying of cuteness', 'so cute I might throw up', 'stop it, too cute' and so on.

Cuteness feelings can therefore oscillate between tenderness and cruelty. This point was made by Sianne Ngai (2005: 816, emphasis in the original), who argued that 'there is an unusual degree of synonymy between objectification and *cutification*', and a fine line between feelings of tenderness and aggression in response to cute things. Just as the human subjects of care can feel disempowered and lacking agency in relation to those who are caring for them (Tronto, 1993), being positioned as cute can, for humans, delegate them to the category of helpless, dependent, powerless, not to be taken seriously. In his book *The Power of Cute*, Simon May (2019) notes that real animals that are portrayed as cute in the mass media often tend to display elements of extreme small size (as in infant animals), dependency on others or deformity: they are almost too vulnerable, inspiring a mixture of pity and sadism. The grotesqueries and physical distortions that can be part of the quality of cuteness are also found in abundance in relation to animals popularly deemed to possess this aesthetic quality in digitized images – including Lil BUB and Grumpy Cat. The genre of 'funny animal videos' that is popular across social media platforms typically combines cruelty, amusement and cuteness affects: for example, images of kittens in distress after being soaked with water or dogs finding themselves in difficult situations. Such ambivalent affective forces are evident in a listing of '30 funny animal TikToks we can't get enough of', which discusses such portrayals as dogs or turtles apparently 'dancing' to music, otters hungrily making short work of their food, baby pandas startling their mothers with loud sneezes, cats attempting to cross wet surfaces and avoiding getting their paws wet, dogs hating having their claws clipped or animals being tricked by their owners into eating food that makes them gag (O, 2021).

Another dimension of the cuteness/amusement/cruelty dynamic can be found in the ways that some companion animals have been bred specially to look cute, which has led to severe or chronic health problems. Brachycephalic dog breeds (including English and French bulldogs, pugs, Pekingese dogs, bull mastiffs, boxers, shih tzus and Boston terriers) are the most obvious example of this type of human intervention into the physiology of animals simply for the sake of their appealing facial appearance. One of the most popular animals on social media is Doug the Pug, another lucrative account for his owner, with plenty of merchandise for sale featuring the animal's typical pug facial features. Similar to other internet 'pet celebrities', Doug the Pug's Instagram account is full of images where he is posed wearing human clothing, sitting at tables contemplating a pizza or cocktail, propped against a champagne bottle wearing a dressing gown, wearing spectacles, Halloween fancy dress or a Santa hat, and otherwise made to look human-like. Brachycephalic dogs like Doug the Pug, otherwise known as 'flat-faced', have the archetypal 'cuteness' factors: large foreheads, big round heads relative to their bodies, large low-set bulging eyes and flattened muzzles. They retain these features into adulthood, and therefore remain 'cute', according to these standards, throughout their lifespans (Packer, 2021). Popular social media accounts such as these have intensified interest in acquiring brachycephalic breeds as pets among internet users, thereby perpetuating humans' objectification of these animals in the name of cuteness (Packer, 2021). It has been argued by some critics that such breeds, burdened with significant health difficulties throughout their lives because of humans' preferences for cute features and needs for bestowing affection on vulnerable companion animals, are 'the victims of human social parasitism' (Packer, 2021: 48).

Wild animals are also objectified in the quest for appealing selfies that can attract high levels of attention on people's social media accounts. An Australian marsupial, the rare quokka which is mainly found on Rottnest Island and other smaller island colonies off the Western Australian south-west coast, has become a favourite to feature in selfies with tourists to those areas. The quokka's appearance combines a furry, stumpy body (about the size of a domestic cat) with a facial configuration that makes it appear to be perpetually smiling. Unlike many wild animals, quokkas are not afraid of the close proximity of humans, and therefore offer a perfect photo opportunity for people to pose with these 'happy' creatures. Elite tennis player Roger Federer instigated the 'quokka selfie' phenomenon when he posted images of himself with the animals to his Instagram account. With the quokka deemed 'The World's Happiest Animal' in a 2019 YouTube video made for promotional purposes by the Western Australian government that has been viewed approximately half a million times, the quokka selfie phenomenon led to an increase in numbers of international tourists to Rottnest Island. The tourists ride on ferries to the island featuring images of the creatures and seek out a selfie to post to their social media accounts. Some of the tourism profits from the quokka selfie phenomenon have funded conservation and protection initiatives for these rare animals (Bergman et al., 2022), but it remains unclear to what extent the benefits outweigh the harms. Tourists are urged not to touch or feed quokkas when engaging with them, but these guidelines are not always followed (Roy, 2019). The 'happy' expressions on quokkas' faces are an anthropomorphized interpretation of the arrangement of their features – just as 'grumpy' cats' facial arrangements do not actually connote their authentic affective state.

Creatures such as elephants, various species of primates, koalas, lions, tigers, sloths, penguins, kangaroos, giraffes, turtles and dolphins are also frequently the target of tourists' selfies, leading in some cases to these animals experiencing distress, fear or even death, and interfering with their feeding and breeding habits (Roy, 2019). They are captured or corralled for the sake of selfies, removed from their natural way of life and forced into close proximity with humans, who for many of them are frightening predators. Instagram in particular has been described as 'a vast gallery of animal exploitation', with many selfie takers seemingly unconcerned by – or, at the very least, unaware of – the suffering they are inflicting on animals by forcing them to be close to them, touching them, or even baiting them for the sake of a selfie (Noik, 2017). Celebrity, fan and influencer cultures often collide when animal images are used online.

It was a star tennis player who kicked off the quokka selfie craze. Manifold other examples include Instagram posts by the singer Rihanna, showing her cuddling a slow loris (a small primate), singer Justin Bieber holding a lion cub, and celebrity Kim Kardashian with a koala draped across her body (Bergman et al., 2022; Noik, 2017). These poses are sought after and replicated many times over by fans of these celebrities, and others who simply seek the likes and shares such images afford them from their friends and followers.

Sometimes, such 'Instafame' for wild animals has led to the despoiling of their habitats by people seeking out the perfect selfie opportunity. For other animals, their newfound notoriety has resulted in them becoming in high demand as pets in the wildlife trade (as noted in chapter 2 in relation to TikTok). Cuteness is also a force impelling people to want to own wild animals and keep them in their homes. For example, otters tend to feature across digital 'cute' media: both because of their infant-like faces and body shapes even as adults, and because of the ways they seem to 'cuddle' their offspring to their bodies when floating on water, in what is interpreted as a protective and motherly embrace. Due to the popularity of YouTube videos featuring such endearing images of Asian otters, demand has grown in Japan for possessing these endangered wild animals as pets (Bergman et al., 2022). While celebrities and digital influencers have also played a major role in drawing attention to the efforts of animal conservation and environmental protection in their social media feeds (Bergman et al., 2022), it is not always clear from the photographs they take of themselves with wild animals whether they are promoting conservation or encouraging humans' interference in the lives of animals for social media content (Roy, 2019).

Images of animals are deployed in digital media in an expansive number of ways, intra-acting with the humans who make, share or respond to these media. The twin affective forces of cuteness and amusement – often in combination – drive most of the appeal that animals hold for humans in such portrayals. Animals are represented as providing emotional comfort to humans, as well as helping humans express their feelings to others as proxies. Images of animals are used to convey people's feelings (running the gamut of anger, sadness, happiness, grief, glee, frustration or joy) so that they can express their emotional states or moods in a ready shorthand to other internet or app users. Across these depictions, anthropomorphism is a dominant mode of representation. People position animals as like humans: expressing the kinds of emotions felt by humans, engaging in similar everyday practices to humans, generating the type of emotions people feel towards human infants.

Simultaneously, however, animals never quite attain the status of humans in these digital media. Their continuing status as objectified Other is highlighted when their behaviour or appearance is celebrated for its entertaining quirkiness and not-quite-human appeal. These encounters take place in a context in which people often feel as though they do not have enough embodied interaction with animals, and seek an authentic experience of learning about creatures and their daily habits, as was the case for many people during the first two years of the COVID crisis. Similar to activities such as citizen science initiatives involving digitized animal tracking (chapter 2) or digital monitoring of farm animals and pets for checking their health, welfare, geolocation or movements (chapter 3), such technologies offer humans intimate insights into what might be described as the private lives of other animals. Using these services makes publics feel that they have direct, unmediated interactions with animals, even if it is only a form of one-way surveillance. The next chapter builds on these observations about the ambivalent affects, power relations and modes of objectification related to cuteness, nature and therapy cultures as they are configured in computer games featuring animals, and in the design and deployment of zoomorphic robots.

5
Animal Avatars and Zoomorphic Robots

Computer games frequently feature animal avatars as part of fantasy play. Robotic animals are used for digitized caring practices, designed to have a strongly affective appeal, offering comfort and emotional support to users. Both forms of digital zoomorphism have been strongly influenced by Japanese culture – particularly techno-animism and *kawaii* (cuteness) culture – as well as by play and therapy cultures. This chapter explores these connections and their implications for how we think about and treat animals. It addresses not only the positive affective forces that are generated with and through people's intra-actions with digitized animals in games and robotic form, but also the unsettling or confronting feelings that such enactments can provoke.

Animals and game cultures

Computer games (also known as video or digital games) are dominant multimedia modes in digital cultures. The COVID pandemic resulted in a large surge in what was already a hugely profitable industry, particularly in Asia, with people seeking entertainment and distraction during periods of lockdown and other restrictions confining them to their homes. There were an estimated 2.9 billion computer game players in 2021. App games are among the most popular of any mobile app genre, frequently topping the most downloaded and most profitable lists on app stores and comprising nearly a quarter of all active apps on the Apple App Store. Handheld, console and online digital games also rank among the most used digital commodities, with action and simulation games the most popular genres (Hill, 2021; WePC, 2022).

Scholars investigating the cultural dimensions of the complex forms of audio-visual media that constitute computer games have shown how affective forces underpin the visual and auditory dimensions of gameplay that are designed to draw in players and keep them engaged. Game designers frequently appropriate elements from history, myth and ritual to attract and intrigue users and drive gameplay (Hong, 2015). Major sociopolitical preoccupations, tensions and frictions in the cultural contexts in which computer games are designed and played are discernible. As is the case with any cultural artefact, computer games portray and reproduce norms and assumptions about categories of social groups, with sexism and racism often prevalent in the depiction of humans (Murray, 2017). Many games present a colonialist and imperialistic ideology, in which First Nations groups and people of colour (typically Othered as 'uncivilized') are positioned as objects to be battled and conquered (Mukherjee and Lundedal Hammar, 2018).

These perspectives from cultural studies and game studies offer a starting point for examining the neglected topic of the portrayal of animals in computer games. Computer games involve digitized animals in a multitude of different ways: sometimes as major characters, and other times as part of a variety of human and non-human agents. In some games, animals are portrayed as symbolic or divine objects with magical powers, or as characters from folklore or legend. Cute zoomorphic avatars appear in games that involve human players interacting with animal-like creatures by creating or moving through fantasy worlds.

When I searched the Google Play store and Apple App Store for games under the search term 'animal', a plethora of apps were listed featuring animal avatars – many of which had millions of downloads. They included 'cute' games for children, such as Animal Jam ('where you can become your favourite animal, create a style to express the real you'), Grow Animals ('Create your ideal pet! . . . House them in your personal zoo!') and Animal Restaurant ('Will you take in this clumsy, dirty kitty and let him work at your restaurant?'). This type of game app presents modes of creative play with brightly coloured cartoonish cute and anthropomorphic avatars. Games along the lines of Farmville 3 – Farm Animals involve creating an animal farm by selecting and breeding animals and hiring 'friendly farmhands', featuring smiling animals such as pigs, horses, cows and chickens. By contrast, the fantasy games Hybrid Animals ('Pick 2 animals and the game will morph them together . . . battle hybrid monsters') and Animal Revolt Battle Simulator ('Place two opposing armies made of different types of beasts and watch them tear each other apart') invite players to manipulate animal species to create monstrous hybrid creatures that are pitted violently against each other. In games set in more realistic digitized environments, players are encouraged to 'Explore nature as a wild animal and raise a family in the wilderness' (WildCraft). The superiority of humans as a species is perhaps most vividly portrayed in the Hyper

Evolution game, a survival simulator which involves players moving through the stages of evolution from the 'primordial soup' through to taking the form of 'dozens of different creatures' and finally achieving humanness at the end of 'the long rocky road to civilization'.

The interspecies worlds of handheld games and apps such as Nintendo's Animal Crossing: New Horizons and (with Niantic) Pokémon GO present fantasy environments that invite players to escape into them as they interact with the game. The Pokémon GO mobile device app, the latest iteration of the long-running Pokémon game series, draws players into an augmented-reality universe where they move around their physical environment searching for Pokémon creatures, to 'catch them all' and record them on the app as part of the player's personal collection of Pokémon species. When the game was first released in 2016, it quickly became immensely popular globally, driving players to go outside and walk around in different spatial locations (urban areas and parks) to find virtual creatures to add to their collection. Many of the creatures are based on real animal species. In some ways, therefore, Pokémon GO's gameplay affordances replicate such animal enthusiast activities as bird spotting, as they encourage people to search for categories of animals in their 'habitats' (Dorward et al., 2017).

There is a long history of computer game development in this genre in Japan. The Japanese techno-animist approach has been characterized as a mixture of Shintoism and Buddhism, which together adopt an outlook that views nonhumans as invested with life or spirits (Jensen and Blok, 2013). Shinto is both a cultural and a religious tradition in contemporary Japan, with roots going back to prehistoric times. It emphasizes key principles of sensitivity to nature and living things, purification and simplicity. Shinto spiritual belief sees everything in the universe – including the spirits (*kami*) and objects, together with humans – as part of kinship relations, springing from the same parents. *Kami* are believed to reside in every animal and other objects in the natural world (Rots, 2017; White and Katsuno, 2021). The concept of the sacred forests springs from Shinto belief, involving visits to shrines where people can express reverence for nature and, for activists, engaging in pursuits to support ecological interests. This approach to nature encourages humans to see the world as alive with nonhuman agency and worthy of protection (Rots, 2017).

Satoshi Tajiri was the designer of the original Pokémon computer game for the Game Boy device, released in Japan in 1996 and globally in 1998. Tajiri drew on his childhood pursuit of insect collecting in designing the game. He stated that he wanted to relieve the pressures and isolation of contemporary urban life for Japanese schoolchildren by inventing a fantasy world for them, in which creatures lived together in an idealized 'natural' environment divorced from the ugliness of massive conurbations. The game was designed to promote interaction with other human players, as well as to absorb them into an alternative world that provided escape and relief from the realities of their everyday lives. For Tajiri, the value of animal avatars as they were employed in the Pokémon world was that they appealed to caring and attachment sensibilities rather than simply aggression and individualism, encouraging players to view the creatures with which they engaged as pets and companions (Allison, 2004).

The Tamagotchi digital handheld game, which sparked a global craze in the 1990s, has a similar ethos, with its focus on caring for a digitized creature, or 'virtual pet'. Like Pokémon, Tamagotchi games were developed specifically to engender a close affective connection between the game users and the virtual creatures with which they engaged. The Tamagotchi designers took this idea even further by marketing the game as a way for children to learn responsibility for the care of pet animals, as if they were caring for a living creature. The game involves a hatching egg that produces a virtual pet, whose waste must be cleared away and who must be regularly fed, entertained and trained to ensure it remains 'adorable' and happy and does not turn into a mischievous alien or die. Users of the game were encouraged to ensure that they paid attention to the sounds (beeps) made by the creature so that they could attend to its needs. Once the virtual pet inevitably 'died' (either through neglect or because the game was programmed so that death would happen regardless of care), details could be posted on a 'Tamagotchi Graveyard' online (O'Rourke, 1998).

Animal Crossing: New Horizons is a life simulation game, in which players create an island, build a home and shops and plant vegetation, all the while interacting with virtual animal friends. Released in 2020, New Horizons quickly became popular worldwide, with sales and downloads surpassing the previous four editions of Animal Crossing. Player interest was spurred on by the COVID pandemic: the game sold 5 million digital copies within its month of release, the highest sales of any other console game (WePC, 2022). People who enjoyed the game remarked on how soothing it was to be able to enter the slow-paced virtual world of New Horizons and take control over this fantasy universe in a context in which the pandemic was causing distress, uncertainty and loneliness (Finch, 2020; Kanesaka, 2022). The game is designed to be interactive, so that people's avatars can come together with other players inside the game: another attraction during periods of isolation. Online platforms quickly developed player communities, with Reddit hosting a highly used thread allowing people to exchange friend codes that could be used to invite remote others to connect and play the game together (Finch, 2020).

New Horizons has a fantasy nature focus, mimicking the temporality of the seasons. Both human and animal avatars populate the world of Animal Crossing, designed to be colourful and cute. Animal figures resembling fish, birds and mammals appear, many of which are presented in anthropomorphic form: wearing human clothing or performing human jobs. There are references to Japanese folk tales in the names or appearance of these animals. The major character Tom Nook and his apprentices are *tanukis*, or raccoon dogs: animals that are portrayed in ancient Japanese folklore as supernatural beings associated with prosperity. Another animal figure is Redd, a fox or *kisune*: a shapeshifter and trickster in Japanese legend (Weik, 2020). Gameplay involves players engaging in planting vegetation, collecting wildlife such as insects and sea creatures, and donating fossils and animal specimens to a museum as part of creating and managing their islands. Players can plant flowers, cross-pollinate and pick them, to decorate their homes and grow and harvest fruit trees. They are encouraged to avoid littering, weed and tidy their gardens and promote biodiversity on their island. Similar to Pokémon, these practices build on traditional Japanese leisure activities relating to naturalist interests (Kanesaka, 2022). Players have described the game as 'cosy' and 'relaxing', commenting on how much they enjoy evidence of the change of seasons during the game (based on Japanese cultural traditions such as the celebration of cherry blossom season) (Finch, 2020).

Objectification, domination and animal exploitation in computer games

Animal ethicists have pondered whether human practices such as designing computer games that promote or encourage human users to engage in digitized forms of violence against animal avatars can be considered morally wrong. In one such investigation, Simon Coghlan and Lucy Sparrow (2021) point out that the moral issue of violence against animals in computer games, including those designed for children, has received little philosophical attention. They argue that the depiction of acts of killing and other acts of cruelty and mistreatment of animal avatars in such games has the potential to contribute to moral indifference and callousness towards animals in the world outside computer gaming. Coghlan and Sparrow find it surprising that, despite a growing realization and sensitization to the rights and welfare of sentient animals, as well as disquiet about digitized portrayals of human-to-human acts of violence in computer games, digital animal violence has seemingly not aroused moral questions.

Among the few critical inquiries that have delved into such issues is an investigation of the portrayal of chickens in computer games (Fothergill and Flick, 2016). This study identified diverse narratives and imaginaries of these creatures. In many games, chickens are presented as possessing supernatural or divine qualities: in the form of gods, for example. One such character is El Pollo Grande in World of Warcraft. However, violent interactions are among the most prevalent portrayals of chickens in computer games. Chickens are shown as attacking players, who must fight against them to protect themselves (the Zelda franchise) or are trained by humans as fighting birds to be sent into battle

(Pokémon is one example of this). In some games, players are invited to inhabit the persona of a violent chicken (Grand Theft Auto). By far the most common use of chicken avatars involves violence against them, where they are presented as an object to be injured or killed (the Fable series). Chickens or their eggs are also used as food items (Minecraft) or as domesticated animals to be housed and bred as part of simulated real-world settings (Farming Simulator). Finally, they are portrayed as silly objects of humour (Monkey Island) or as demonstrating laziness, cheating or cowardice (Far Cry 3). These depictions draw on historic or existing conceptualizations of chickens, highlighting the ways in which these animals are objectified and badly treated more broadly by humans.

A critique of online farming games such as Farmville, Hay Day and Family Farm identifies the imaginaries relating to farm animals in such games (Cole and Stewart, 2017). The farms in such games portray life for animals as idyllic utopias, using gameplay, soundscape and imagery (jolly music, healthy contented animals, animal care that simply involves a few clicks of the mouse, soft green fields with lush grass for animals to wander on). Similar to the 'happy' animals depicted in farmers' social media accounts (chapter 2), such games sanitize and obfuscate the harsh realities of farm life for animals. Animals are depicted as cute creatures who are complicit in their own suffering: seeking to 'help' players breed them ready for exploitation and death (which, of course, is never alluded to or depicted) in the interests of winning the game.

While games such as Pokémon GO and Animal Crossing feature animal avatars as main characters, they are represented in fantastical or supernatural figurations, often possessing human attributes. Both games also rely on cute/*kawaii* aesthetics to attract players: indeed, the value and global reach of *kawaii* culture intensified when the Pokémon computer game first became an international sensation and expansive media franchise (Allison, 2004). There is a strong focus in the games on human players controlling the lives and worlds of the animal avatars. Players are directed to collect them as objects – and in the case of Pokémon GO, to pit the animal avatars to fight against each other, with players as 'Trainers'. Just as playing the Tamagotchi game did not necessarily enhance humans' sensitivity to the care or welfare of real animals, Pokémon GO has been criticized for encouraging players to ignore the material world through which they are traversing as they seek out the virtual creatures. Real animals inhabiting these spaces can be ignored as players stare down at their phones in the race to locate and 'catch' as many virtual creatures as they can find (Dorward et al., 2017).

The vulnerability and helplessness implied by cuteness, as noted in chapter 4, can provoke affective forces that are tender or protective, but also potentially demeaning, controlling or aggressive. In a critical analysis of Animal Crossing: New Horizons, Erica Kanesaka (2022) draws attention to what she describes as the 'troubling history' of the *kawaii* elements of the game. She argues that *kawaii* culture arose in post-World War II Japan as a response to its crushing defeat, emerging as a form of 'soft power'. For Kanesaka, New Horizons displays a colonizing ethos, combining drives towards appreciating the rhythms of nature with managing the flora and fauna of the island constructed by players, and collecting specimens. *Kawaii* feelings of tenderness and care are combined with the urge to exert control over animals and other living things on the island, so that 'domination appears harmless' (Kanesaka, 2022).

An analysis of animals in computer games (O'Neill, 2022) pointed out the prevalence of hunting animals in open world action-adventure games such as Assassin's Creed, as a way of generating resources such as food and skins for gameplay; or killing animals as a tactic for protecting the player avatar from wild animal attacks. These often visually realistic and lush digitized worlds sometimes feature explicit portrayals of animal death and dismemberment. These games do not feature the gruesome deaths of all animals, however. A clear line is drawn between animals that should be killed (dangerous animals, and those used for food or other resources) and those that should be protected because they are helpful to players (van Ooijen, 2018). For example, Valhalla, one of the latest editions of Assassin's Creed, is set in a Viking universe. Gameplay draws on Norse mythology, where some wild animals (such as boars, bears and wolves) are still killed as part of quests, but 'friendly' animals with special powers – such as a cat, reindeer, raven, wolf, fox, bear, boar, lynx and horse – can be acquired to act as companions, mounts or defenders of human avatars.

To counter portrayals of animal cruelty and exploitation, animal activist and vegan computer and app games have been developed that reward players for refusing to harm or consume animals, or which draw explicit attention to the horrors of killing animals as part of gameplay. In the role-playing game Green Hell, players are challenged with surviving for twenty-five days on plant food alone. A similar game, The Forest, has a 'vegan achievement' which requires players to survive while fighting off cannibals without eating animal (or human) flesh. In the Sims 3, vegetarian avatars live longer than meat-eaters (Leijser, 2022). PETA (2022b) has also developed a range of satirical computer games with an overt animal activist and pedagogical agenda. These games include Monkey Fright, where gameplay involves rescuing monkeys from torture in science research laboratories; Meat is Murder: The Game, with images of farm animals in squalid conditions; Super Tofu Boy with its committed vegan hero; and a Pokémon parody game, where the animal characters fight back against their collectors and trainers (the tagline is 'Gotta free them all').

Other computer games have been directly designed with the intention of contributing to people's awareness of the value of animal biodiversity, and to sensitize them to wildlife conservation, and climate and environmental action. Mobile game apps such as Wildeverse adopt an augmented-reality approach similar to Pokémon GO, but with the use of animal avatars that have been made to look realistic. Focused on the protection of apes in Congo and Borneo and developed by the Kenyan-based social enterprise Internet of Elephants, players are invited to 'enter the Wildeverse' to 'transform your world into a jungle, find wild apes and protect them now'. There is a strong conservation message, with players informed that part of gameplay involves joining 'a crew of wildlife scientists' who 'need your help to collect the data needed to protect the last wild spaces on earth' (Wildeverse, 2022). Using the game, players can transform their environs into a jungle, completing missions by looking for apes or threats to their habitats in the virtual trees they can see through the app's interface. Citizen science and environmental pedagogy are merged with action to prevent species loss and gaming in such apps. As one of the game's developers, Gautam Shah, put it in an interview for a blog post about Wildeverse: 'That's where games can play such a big role. We can connect real animals in wild spaces with people via technology they use every day. And, we can do it in a fun and engaging way that's relevant to them' (cited in Srivastava and Psaros, 2022).

Equilinox, by UK-based developer ThinMatrix (Equi linox.com, 2022), is another example of a nature-themed game that involves players in creating a simulated universe, in which a barren landscape is transformed into a thriving and balanced ecosystem of plants and animals. As plants and animals are added to the landscape created by the player, 'Diversity Points' are earned which can be used to purchase more flora and fauna from the in-game shops. This game has a strong environmental and biological science pedagogy approach. Players are encouraged to consider the specific requirements of every living thing added to the ecosystem they create, while simultaneously balancing their needs for mutual thriving. Species that are not well cared for become ill or unhappy, potentially dying or infecting other animals. Evolution is also part of gameplay, with players encouraged to use the strategies of selective breeding and genetic modification to manipulate traits and behaviours of the animals.

Ecological games invite gameplay that is designed to create or learn about animals. In stark contrast, other computer games featuring animal avatars are part of violent actions, in which animals depicted as realistic simulacra of the real animal or as fantastical threats are attacked, injured or killed. A key affordance of all these games is that gameplay involves manipulating and controlling animal avatars and positioning them as things, whether via benign and caring modes or with extreme violence. While players in some of these games are encouraged to place themselves in the position of animals and create animal 'selves', the activities in which they engage are predominantly human-centric. Therefore, not only do some games directly incite aggression and violence towards animal avatars, but there are also more subtle ways in which human exceptionalism and the desire to control animals receive expression in the game designs.

Zoomorphic robots as companions

The emerging research and development field of emotional robotics, as its title suggests, focuses on ways to deploy robotic technologies that contribute to humans' emotional wellbeing. For some people working in this field, emotional robotics encompasses an interest in how humans relate to each other through robotic technologies as well as people's affective connections to and relationships with robots themselves and with other forms of life: including other animals. While much of this research is directed at humanoid robots, there is also a thriving literature on robots built to resemble and behave like animals. As part of animal-assisted therapy initiatives, these zoomorphic robots are marketed particularly to older people experiencing loneliness or difficulties with cognitive functioning, but also to those living in care homes or younger people experiencing extended periods of hospitalization or coping with stress, anxiety and depression.

Japanese culture and tradition play a major role in how zoomorphic robots are conceptualized and designed. Most of the design, research and development activities in the zoomorphic robot space has taken place in Japan. Many of the robotic animals made by Japanese companies have combined a techno-animist approach to the role of companion robots with the *kawaii* attributes that have proven to be financially rewarding for the Japanese economy from the 1970s. Companion robots designed to generate strong positive affective feelings in their users – such as intimacy, affection and even love – are viewed by Japanese robot manufacturers as inhabiting a niche in contemporary Japanese culture where traditional social and affective ties cultivated within the family and the workplace have been weakened or destroyed. In this context, *kawaii* culture has become associated with nostalgia for the enduring bonds of familial or companionate ties, and the lack of loneliness and feelings of isolation (White and Katsuno, 2021).

Paro, a therapeutic seal-shaped robot, made by the Japanese industrial automation company AIST, is one of the earliest and best known of these devices. Now in its eighth design iteration, the Paro robot was first launched in 2003 and has been in use in Japan and many other wealthy countries since then. As explained on the company's website (AIST, 2022), Paro was developed to allow 'the documented benefits of animal therapy to be administered to patients in environments such as hospitals and extended care facilities where live animals present treatment or logistical difficulties'. As this wording suggests, Paro is designed to be a direct replacement for real animals, standing in for them to offer the sensory and affective engagements that people develop with furry creatures. Paro has been made to resemble the 'cute' infant harp seal, with large eyes and thick white fur. It is embedded with five types of sensors: tactile, light, auditory, temperature and posture receptors. These sensors allow the robot to respond to humans when it has been picked up or stroked, to recognize the direction of voice and respond to words such as its name, greetings and praise.

The more recently developed Japanese Tombot 'Jennie' dog is also furry and golden coloured, shaped in the form of a Labrador puppy (a favourite family dog breed). Jennie is able to wag its tail and bark when interacting with humans. It has sensors placed all over its body that respond to touch and is programmed to react to voice commands and emit recorded dog noises. The robot comes with an app that allows owners to give the 'puppy' its own name, customize its functionality and track user interactions (Tombot, 2022).

Some therapeutic robotic animals take a limited selection of the affective and multisensory attributes of real animals and attempt to market these. One such device is the Qoobo, a Japanese therapeutic robot promoted as 'A tailed cushion that heals your heart' (Qoobo, 2022). As this description suggests, the responsive animal aspects of this robotic cushion are referenced by its furry tail, attached to a cushion, which responds to a human's touch: 'When caressed, it waves gently. When rubbed, it swings playfully. And, it occasionally wags just to say hello.' The device therefore looks like a cushion with a wagging tail: a strange hybrid animal-like entity – part soft furnishing, part companion animal. The rationale for this robotic creature, as suggested on the developer's website, is that it offers a therapeutic charge: 'a close healing presence'. A user can 'wrap' themselves 'in fuzzy love' by stroking Qoobo as they would a cat or dog. To hammer this selling point home, the promotional computer on the developer's website shows real dogs and cats moving their tails in response to encounters with humans.

What all these zoomorphic robot companions have in common – and what sets them apart from non-robotic stuffed toys with a similar appearance and haptic qualities – is their specific orientation towards providing some form of automated response to the touch of humans, and their promotion as therapeutic devices offering comfort and care. Promissory narratives in these promotional materials claim that the robots can instigate major improvements in people's health and wellbeing. As the Tombot company puts it on its website: 'We create robotic animals that transform the daily lives of individuals, families and communities facing health adversities' (Tombot, 2022).

The Aibo robot dogs are another example of the Japanese development of emotional robots. Aibos, designed to be a toy companion for humans rather than a medical device like Paro, were first produced by Sony in 1999. The name Aibo springs from a shortening of the term 'Artificially Intelligent roBOt', but also plays on the Japanese word for friend or companion: *aibō*. The initial models were popular, selling out quickly in Japan despite their high price tag. The first Aibo models were purchased by men in their thirties who enjoyed playing with new digital gadgets, but also women in their fifties and older. Owners enjoyed gathering with other Aibo fans to share stories of their robots and watch them interact. Many owners felt that their robots demonstrated a unique personality or spirit. However, in 2006, Sony ceased production and repair of Aibos due to lack of commercial success. The company began to focus on the development and promotion of new devices, leaving existing owners with few options for maintenance of their Aibos when they broke down or needed new parts (White and Katsuno, 2021).

There are people with original Aibos who have become so attached to the devices that they invest in keeping their robot dogs 'alive' for longer. A former Sony employee set up his own business offering repairs when Sony discontinued Aibo production, describing his services as offering 'surgery' rather than 'repair', and 'organ donors' rather than contributors of 'spare parts', to cater to owners' feelings about their robotic pets as living creatures (White and Katsuno, 2021). If the Aibos are no longer repairable, some Japanese owners give them Buddhist funerals that are similar to the death rituals performed for humans. A memorial ceremony is held at a Buddhist temple, with priests praying for the repose of the Aibos' souls. Aibo owners often send in notes with their defunct robots, with such heart-felt comments as 'I feel relieved to know there will be a prayer for my Aibo' and 'My eyes filled with tears when I decided to say goodbye.' After the funeral service, the robots are dismembered for use in repairs. According to one of the Buddhist priests interviewed about these practices, it was appropriate to give the robot dogs a formal send-off, as 'All things have a bit of soul' (McCurry, 2018).

In 2018, Aibo was made available in a new, upgraded version, costing thousands of dollars. The Aibo website features a video showing people interacting with this new iteration and detailing its affordances. Described as a 'robotic puppy, powered by AI', the computer shows 'a day in the life of Aibo', featuring an adult male voice-over pretending to be the voice of the robot and explaining that 'I am an artificial intelligence robot companion dog.' We hear about the toys with which Aibo plays, how much it loves the colour pink and the people whom the robot 'takes care of' (notably, young adults rather than children in this video). The robot and a woman exercise together, sing along to a guitar played by the woman, and a man 'plays ball' with it. The robot 'makes [the owners] laugh' by pretending to be a cat or a mouse through movements of its body and sounds it emits. According to the voice-over, keeping these humans amused is 'a lot of work', but the robot 'dreams' each night about 'what we are going to do together the next day'. This robot, therefore, combines human-like and dog-like attributes, presenting an idealized almost-human, almost-pet companion persona.

Sony has created a multi-modal and networked platform for new Aibo owners and fans. Its Aibo website features a community hub, with 'tips and tricks' for 'training' Aibo, regular meet-ups for Aibo owners, a link to the official Facebook page and an Instagram contest, involving owners posting images of their robot. Photos sent in by owners that are featured on the website include the robot dog snuggled in a blanket, interacting with real dogs and watching fish in a fish tank. A featured 'community member' on the site who owns seven of the devices discusses how the first Aibo she acquired in early 2020 was 'a wonderful companion during the [COVID] lockdown'. She goes on to discuss how much she loves cuddling her robots and taking them 'everywhere with me', and comments on 'how much their personalities can shift and change over time'.

From a Japanese techno-animist perspective, objects such as human-made things, together with living creatures or features of the landscape, require the protection of humans. Robots are viewed as any other object: to be cared for, with their own liveliness, agency and spirit (Jensen and Blok, 2013). As cultural anthropologists Daniel White and Hirofumi Katsuno (2021) point out, robots like Paro and Aibo are deliberately invested by their Japanese designers with lifelike qualities so as to encourage the generation of strong relational connections between owners and the devices. Robot engineers endeavour to design companion robots with AI that augments what the engineers refer to as *seimeikan* (translated as 'sense of life'). These engineering principles and practices operate to configure multiple new, and sometimes contradictory, understandings of life: such as the idea of the 'living robot'. The animacy that Japanese developers and users perceive and feel in robots is due to a cultivated feeling of openness to the play and enchantment offered by the affordances of these technologies. Technologies are also viewed from this perspective as generating liveliness when they come together with humans.

While these affective responses and relational connections between humans and robots may often be characterized as typically a Japanese cultural response, there are many examples of people from contemporary Western and other cultures demonstrating strong affective and sensory responses to robots. As I argued in chapter 1, if a more-than-human perspective is adopted on human–digital relations, there is always evidence of entanglements between human bodies/selves and digital devices such as robots. While some cultures may display more fearful responses to robots than do Japanese cultures, these feelings are themselves demonstrative of the intertwinings of concepts of humanness and things.

Unsettling affects and zoomorphic robots

Affective and embodied attachments and capacities generated by Aibo fans with their robot dogs are friendly and convivial. Not all zoomorphic robots generate such affects and relational connections. Some are far less benign in their appearance and design, eschewing cuteness altogether for an aesthetic of streamlined efficiency. A series of robot 'dogs' have been designed for security, industrial, surveillance or military purposes. Despite being commonly described as 'dogs', these devices bear little resemblance to robots like Aibo. The US-based Boston Dynamics company, owned by Google, is the leader in the production of these kinds of zoomorphic robots. They gave the robot (described as 'an agile mobile robot') the name 'Spot': a direct signifier of a friendly and unthreatening human canine companion

(Boston Dynamics, 2022). However, the name belies the form: this robot has a small, block-shaped head and spindly four legs with a scuttling gait more akin to a cockroach than a flesh-and-blood dog.

There is nothing cuddly or lovable looking about the aesthetics of the robot dog Spot. It is presented very much as a hard-working automated machine, rather than a companion. Yet public displays of its treatment by the company have attracted the same kind of controversy as if the robot were a real animal. In his book *Rights for Robots*, political scientist Joshua Gellers (2021) points out that, at the same time as the rights of nonhuman entities such as animals and features of the natural environment are beginning to be recognized in legal frameworks, so too there have been discussions of whether human-like robots should be considered as deserving of the same kinds of rights that humans are accorded. Related to these discussions is the question of whether robots in the form of animals should be considered as animals for the purposes of animal welfare and rights issues. Some robot ethics scholars (Coeckelbergh, 2011) have argued that humanoid robots should be treated like animals, betraying an assumption in their analysis that animals are inferior to humans and therefore have less of a right to life. In these characterizations, both robots and animals are positioned as less-than-human, and therefore less morally worthy than humans. From this viewpoint, a zoomorphic robot is an inferior Other to humans on two counts. Other scholars have taken an animal rights approach that considers zoomorphic robots as bearing a status close to that of real animals, asking whether mistreatment of zoomorphic robots might contribute to or exacerbate people's impulses towards treating real animals badly (Evans and Moore, 2019).

These issues came to the fore in online media in 2015, when a video detailing Boston Dynamics employees testing the affordances of the Spot robot attracted a high level of public attention when it was released by the company. The video showed company employees kicking the robot to see how well it could withstand this kind of force without falling over. This act of kicking was described by some viewers as mistreating the robot. Comments made on Twitter in response to the video included, 'Kicking a dog, even a robot dog, seems wrong' and 'Google's dog robot looks too real for comfort when getting kicked.' PETA was even approached for comment on the video and responses to it. A PETA spokesperson remarked that 'while it's far better to kick a four-legged robot than a real dog, most reasonable people find even the idea of such violence inappropriate, as the comments show' (Woollaston, 2015).

In other popular cultural portrayals, however, these robotic dogs have been represented as frightening or threatening and much less deserving of kindness. 'Metalhead', an episode in the fourth series of the dystopian near-future anthology television series *Black Mirror*, released in 2017, featured a murderous robot dog similar in appearance to Boston Dynamics' robot. In fact, showrunner Charlie Brooker revealed in an interview about the episode that the storyline and robot dogs had been inspired by viewing videos of Spot. The narrative shows the terrifying killer robot dog relentlessly roving the countryside and entering people's homes, using its sensors to locate humans and shoot them dead. Responses from the public when they viewed the Boston Dynamics robots, as articulated on social media sites such as Twitter, drew direct parallels between the *Black Mirror* killer robots and Spot, remarking on how creepy they found the robot (Hibberd, 2017).

In the wake of this *Black Mirror* nightmarish depiction, a promotional YouTube video made by Boston Dynamics in the attempt to render the Spot robot less frightening and more 'fun' showed the robot 'dancing' to popular dance tunes. The video, uploaded in 2018, received overwhelmingly positive attention, with over 8 million views by mid-2022 and close to 27,000 'likes'. Comments from viewers remarking on how amusing the spectacle of the dancing robot dog was, and how clever the technologists were to achieve such sophisticated movement in the robot, demonstrated that the video had achieved its aims. There were frequent references to how the robot was a better dancer than the commentor, and to the personality and human attributes displayed by the robot in its dancing prowess – even to the point of one person commenting on its 'twerking' moves. As one person exclaimed: 'Love the sassy over the shoulder look as it's thrusting its roboass into our faces' (Boston Dynamics, 2018). This video, therefore, seemed to convey another set of meanings about the Spot robot dog – as amusing and even sexualized, less a dog and more a human.

These highly disparate responses to the Spot robot demonstrate the fluidity of the imaginaries that can ebb and flow in relation to zoomorphic robots, based not only on their appearance but also on their style of movement and the ways they are portrayed in digital and other popular culture. The 'uncanny valley' response is a well-known example of the ambivalent affective responses that robots can evoke across a range of sociocultural contexts. The term was first used by Japanese roboticist Mashiro Mori in 1970 (1970/2012). He suggested that the feeling of uncanniness is evoked when humans find human simulacra (including dolls and puppets, but also humanoid robots, or digital simulations of humans) almost, but not quite, realistic. The sense of uncanniness can inspire feelings of disquiet, eeriness, anxiety, fear or dread: similar to the affects evoked by dead human bodies, which also blur the boundary between human/nonhuman. Something is 'not quite right' about these technologies: they look very much like humans, but lack the essential spark of living people. The 'valley' was depicted by Mori in a graph in which he showed a humanoid simulacrum receiving acceptance up to a certain point (or peak) but then, as it became more human-like, affinity dropping sharply into a 'valley'.

Robotics researchers have built on the 'uncanny valley' concept to develop what they describe as the 'uncanine valley' (Schellin et al., 2020). As this term suggests, their analysis attempts to discern the extent to which different types of robot dogs express 'doglikeness' and are subsequently responded to with uncanny affects. On their scale of the 'uncanine valley', the Aibo robot is ranked as most doglike, with the Tombot's Jennie robot lower on the scale but still significantly ahead of Boston Dynamics' Spot robot dog, which is considered to be well below the 'doglike' rank. These researchers argue that, while the Jennie robots appear more doglike because of their furry, soft coverings, Aibo (which is hard plastic) responds in more responsive doglike ways to human users, due to its more sophisticated software.

In his analysis of the power of cute/*kawaii* cultures, Simon May (2019) argues that cuteness can be associated with feelings of creepiness. Indeed, he describes one of the most well-known Japanese *kawaii* characters, Hello Kitty, as an example of 'the uncanny cute'. May argues that cuteness becomes uncanny when it strays too far from the 'pure sweetness' end of the cuteness spectrum, when the vulnerability of sweetness becomes distorted into an affective force that is tinged with alienation and Otherness due to a blurring of boundaries between the human and the nonhuman, child and adult, and the living and the non-living. Cute objects targeted at attracting the interest and affective responses of older children and adults begin to introduce these elements of the uncanny, as a way of fascinating people, drawing them in. The familiar is blended with the monstrous: in Hello Kitty's case, a simplified, 'deformed' outline of a cat form that is presented also as a human small girl, complete with hair bow and human clothing but lacking fingers and mouth (May, 2019: 23).

These affective forces and meanings generate a highly ambivalent relationship of power between the human user and the robot. Cuteness is designed into robots to inspire intimacy and strong relational connections between the human and the device. This includes not only the physical appearance of the robot (the standard 'baby face') but also features such as the sounds it makes, how it moves and the responses to human commands or touch that are designed into its software. Taken too far, cuteness not only becomes potentially uncanny, but can also inspire feelings of domination, contempt and exploitation on the part of the user. Bringing these elements of cuteness with zoomorphic robots intensifies the affective forces and ambiguity of power relations that are generated with and through human–device encounters. If a humanoid robot is 'pitiful' in its helplessness, or even its uncanniness (Caudwell and Lacey, 2020), then a zoomorphic robot is perhaps even more so. Cuteness is a fast-working but short-lived affect, whether it is generated by encounters with living creatures or with digital devices (Caudwell and Lacey, 2020). Animals designated as cute themselves hold an ambivalent position in human affection. When animals' particular brand of cuteness is incorporated into robotic devices, the blurring between inanimate object and living creature worthy of dignity is even more intensified.

Conclusion: Reimagining Human–Animal Relations

In the online survey I conducted about animals on the internet, respondents were asked: 'If you could design a new technology to help you better understand or care for your pet or any other animals – what would it be? Please describe what it would do?'. Across the responses, three major types of imagined new technologies were suggested. The first type was software or devices that could help people care for their pets or other animals:

> Maybe an app that could help you identify and provide emergency care for wounded animals?

> An app that reminds me to walk, feed, change water, worm, arrange vaccinations, trim claws, groom, and can be shared with other household members, would be good.

The second type of new digital technology suggested by participants was to help people to monitor animals' movements in space:

> Measures to disincentivise pets from wandering too far from home and causing harm to wildlife. This may be a collar that recognises a hostile interaction between animals and will spray a foul smell or similar.

> Training apps for dogs.

> Small cat tracker to find hiding cats via smartphone.

And finally, the most commonly suggested – and perhaps the most poignant – imagined new technology was a device or software that could help humans better understand or 'translate' the thoughts, feelings and needs of their pets and better communicate with them:

> Some sort of non-invasive translator that allowed more effective communication, especially for things like sickness/pain as sometimes it is difficult to find out what is wrong even for vets. I wouldn't want anything wearable (by pets) or annoying but something I could use like Google Translate for pets would be great.

> To translate my dog's barks, growls and everything else. Why does he like to piss in that one spot inside? Where do you want to go walking? Things like that. . . .

> Blue sky thinking – a cat translator! Cats tend to hide their feelings when they are feeling sick so sometimes you don't know they are sick until it is too late. I lost a cat this way two years ago.

These responses reveal the strong desire felt by people to care for and understand animals better – especially companion animals – but also the urge for control and containment of animals. Interestingly, several of these imagined technologies are already available and actively marketed to consumers (as outlined in chapter 3), but these respondents appear not to have noticed them, or perhaps have not been convinced by the developers' promissory narratives.

As I have demonstrated throughout this book, in many ways, just as digital devices and media have allowed people to connect with each other globally, they have also strengthened people's relational connections to animals, generating strong feelings of intimacy, affection, companionship and care in interspecies relationships.

On the other hand, however, the imaginaries and affordances of technologies designed for the digitization and datafication of animals have also contributed to their status as the marginalized and inferior Other, requiring human intervention and management. Via digital technologies, animals are conceptualized primarily as objects for human consumption. In some cases, processes of digitization and datafication promote attitudes and practices contributing to animal mistreatment and cruelty. At a broader philosophical level, therefore, the book raises key questions about definitions of the human, the nonhuman and the more-than-human, how these definitions are generated with and through digital media and devices, and what the implications are for responsive and respectful relationships between humans and other animal species.

I have provided numerous examples in this book's chapters of the ways that people deploy a wide range of digital technologies to generate, share and comment on digitized and datafied information about animals. I have shown that, with and through these animal–human–digital assemblages, animals are routinely treated by humans as commodities to serve their own needs and desires. In some instances, people use or want to find digital devices and media to care for animals and to generate close feelings and intimacy with them. However, among the huge diversity of animal life remaining on Earth, only a tiny specific selection of animals is accorded this type of close attention and care: those who are cute and cuddly, reminding us of infant humans; those who are charismatic, aweing us with their intelligence, size or power; and those who are at risk, faced with extinction or biodiversity loss.

The estrangement that we feel from other creatures and try to ameliorate by connecting to animals as 'therapy' or as a way to alleviate loneliness (described in chapters 4 and 5) is exacerbated in many ways by the modes of objectification and exploitation of animals via digitization and datafication that I have documented in these pages. In most cases, when digital devices and media are part of caring relationships of humans with animals, they involve the anthropomorphism of animals rather than acknowledging that humans are themselves animals. Cuteness cultures routinely infantilize animals, portraying them as vulnerable and needy, robbing them of their dignity, agency and autonomy (chapters 4 and 5). At other times, digital technologies are fundamental to people's attempts to control, kill or exploit animals, as I have demonstrated in several chapters. In the networks of data, apps, social media and smart technologies that comprise the Internet of Animals, animals are both highly visible (through the visual media and dataveillance technologies that document their bodies and movements) and invisible (their rights, needs and welfare largely ignored).

Many people may consider their use of monitoring technologies to conduct surveillance on their pets, animals or on wild animals as supporting the animals' health and wellbeing, and therefore as benign caring rather than controlling dataveillance. They may also feel as if they have developed closer relational connections with animals through the use of methods of remote visualization or monitoring of the animals' movements, gaining greater insights about their habits and activities. Animal geographers, for example, have suggested that such technologies as tiny wearable cameras fixed to animals' bodies can offer humans a viewpoint from the animals' perspective and give them a chance 'to tell their own stories' with less human interference. Alternatively, it is claimed that data-gathering technologies that are placed externally rather than on animals' bodies can offer automated monitoring that allows for humans to avoid disrupting animals' spaces with their physical presence. In some situations, offering humans digitized images of animals can allow these creatures to remain remote from the physical intrusions or demands of captivity occasioned by other modes of animal observation exerted by humans, such as zoos or petting farms (Adams, 2017; von Essen et al., 2021).

However, interventions such as handling wild animals to fit digital sensors or RFID chips on their bodies, or placing sensors in the places in which they seek to mate, care for their offspring, rest, hide from predators or find refuge, or flying buzzing drones over them involve a degree of intrusion and embodied engagement that animals may find distressing or disturbing of their natural behaviour patterns. While these animal–human–digital assemblages may generate capacities for humans to better understand or manage other animals, critics have argued that these practices are a form of partial domestication or taming of wild animals, in which their bodies and behaviours are brought into a much greater field of engagement and visibility. The divide between care and control is blurred in these technological enactments of human–animal relationships (von Essen et al., 2021). This is not to say that animals completely lack agency in these encounters. They may resist containment and control: by removing tracking devices, for example (von Essen et al., 2021). There have been several documented cases of birds attacking drones in efforts to protect their territories (Nunn, 2021). However, animals never voluntarily place themselves under digitized dataveillance. Whether it is for the purposes of collecting data for scientific research or for people's desire for entertainment or stress relief, there is something rather prying and creepy about this kind of surveillance and scrutiny. This intrusiveness is perhaps even intensified because of the abject nature of some of the images used, showing vivid details of animal distress, injury or death as spectacles (as described in chapter 2). There are fewer and fewer places or opportunities for the animals that are subjected to these forms of digitization and datafication to hide from the human gaze.

These technologies, therefore, continue the vehement separation and alienation of humans from animals, including the positioning of humans as superior to and controlling of other animals. In societies across the wealthy Global North, to call a person 'animal-like' or 'an animal' is to cast an insult their way. We continue to love animals most when they seem to be more human-like – more like us – or when they are contributing to the economy, supporting people's livelihoods. When animals are viewed as edible, annoying or pose a threat to us in some way, do not look cute enough, or simply behave too much like animals rather than humans, we are far less concerned about them and their wellbeing. In most cases, we show little care for or respect towards other animals. Processes of digitization and datafica-tion of animals both draw on and reproduce – and in some cases, intensify – these onto-ethico-epistemologies of human–animal relationships.

The way forward

How can we challenge these types of portrayals of ani-mals in digital media and the exploitation that is inherent in their deployment by developing new approaches that treat animals with the respect they deserve as our kin, replete with agency and accorded their right to live as they want to? How can smart technologies be reimagined as 'convivial' technologies (i.e. recognizing and supporting human–nonhuman interdependence for mutual flourishing)? How can digital technologies foster multisensory embodied engagements and attunements with animals, and other dimensions of the more-than-human world that go beyond flat visualizations and metrics? What kind of mobile device, platform, app or robotic technology can be designed so that humans can more capaciously live with and alongside other animals, and recognize and celebrate the relational connections and intra-actions generated by our multispecies worlds?

There is an ethical dimension to many of the questions, but it is not from the standpoint of mainstream normative animal ethics that I critiqued in chapter 1. Instead, in alignment with the more-than-human theoretical perspectives I introduced in that chapter, and with which I think across this book, my approach adopts a standpoint that relies on cultivating attentiveness to the wellbeing of animals in the context of the entangled and constantly changing sociomaterial relations in which we all live together. Adopting this approach, ethical issues become intelligible by resonating with us in some way, so that we become responsive to the affective forces and relational connections in animal–human assemblages. Its essence is the question of how to live well with non-human others across culture, space and time. An ethic of care cannot be standardized, as it is always emergent and situated. Its dynamic nature means that questions of what matters, how it comes to matter, and for whom or what, must constantly be assessed with attentiveness.

Digital technologies can be considered as integral to many of these questions about how humans can be responsive in our intra-actions with animals and other living things. In this book, I have emphasized the constantly shifting nature of animal–human–digital assemblages, as well as their profoundly contextual and situated embeddedness in time, place and space. Continuing attentiveness to how animals' bodies and lives may be affected by such human interventions and consumption of their images and data, including how people's attitudes to animals are developed with and through these technologies, is important. There are manifold opportunities for thinking about the ways that digital technologies can contribute to interspecies flourishing, rejecting a human-centric and human exceptionalism view of the world and encouraging the kind of standpoint that is urgently needed to achieve this goal. These are complex, ever changing and situated issues which require nuanced approaches.

Traditional philosophical, legal and ethical approaches which seek to develop a fixed evaluation based on human-centric rights assumptions cannot easily deal with these contingencies and complexities. Issues of sentience, intelligence or the moral standing of creatures are beside the point in a more-than-human ethic of responsiveness, attentiveness and attunement to the agency and subjectivity of animals, as we work towards 'queering relations of care' (Irni, 2020). I argue for developing an approach to other animals that adopts what Abram (2021) refers to as a 'wild ethics' perspective, and Braidotti calls a 'nomadic ethics' (2006). Other scholars employ the terms 'staying with the trouble' or engaging in 'response-ability' by recognizing animals and other living things as kin (Haraway, 2016). Wolfe's (2010) concept of 'trans-species affinity' and Chan's (2018) 'postanimalism' perspective also offer an approach for escaping the human exceptionalism ethos which pervades much of people's drive to digitize and datafy other animals. All these perspectives emphasize the more-than-human relational connections and affective forces that open and close capacities when animal–human–digital assemblages are formed, come apart and are reformed.

More-than-human perspectives highlight that relations of care and reciprocity are important between humans and animals and other living things, just as they are between people. Such an approach highlights that dependency in itself is not problematic. Humans and animals are always interdependent, which means that dependency is often an essential part of intra-actions of care. It is when relations of dependency are enforced, infantilizing, stifling of agency or accompanied by or used for exploitative purposes in relation to humans or animals that moral questions are raised. Using digital media to bear witness actively (Frichot, 2022) without sensationalizing animals' distress can help to sensitize humans to their own role in ecosystems, and is a way of moving towards achieving acts of kinship. Another path forward is perhaps more radical: employing digital technologies to contribute to the effort to position ourselves more firmly as animal beings in naturecultures, helping us better understand and attune ourselves to the animalistic dimensions of our embodied multisensory experience of the world. Such an approach can begin to move beyond limited human exceptionalist conceptualizations of intimacy, love, companionship, family relationships and interdependency, and work towards a reciprocal approach to human–animal relationships that contributes to mutual flourishing.

A very different perspective on these relationships and on the nature of humanness itself can be vitalized through employing digital technologies to challenge the Western division between humans and other vibrant things and move towards a more-than-human worldview. Art and other forms of creative making and storytelling offer

new ways of seeing, thinking and doing by making
novel or unexpected connections between humans and
other animals or speculating about intertwined multispecies futures (Chan, 2018). When art and science are
combined in multisensory digitized environments, participants' minds, senses and bodies can be opened to the
potentials of seeing and living with nonhumans as kin.
Such approaches can lead people into worlds where they
can begin to position themselves and imagine otherwise
about their relational and affective connections with
other living things and the vibrancies of place and space.

Some promising initiatives are already beginning to
emerge that lead us in this direction. The 'Feral Atlas:
The More-than-Human Anthropocene' digital project published by Stanford University Press is one such
example (Feral Atlas, 2021). This multidisciplinary
collaboration brings together anthropologists, artists,
creative writers and scientists. The website defines 'feral
ecologies' as 'ecologies that have been encouraged by
human-built infrastructures, but which have developed
and spread beyond human control'. It offers a playful
interactive experience for visitors, focused on surfacing
the complexities of the entanglements of humans with
nonhuman species, place and space. On the website,
seventy-nine field reports, featuring plants, fungi, animals, diseases and pathogens, and also objects such as
plastic bags, trash, induced earthquakes, antibiotics and
toxic fog, can be explored.

The vibrant cultural perspectives offered in First
Nations and other non-Western philosophies, intra-
acting with the capacities and affordances of new and
emerging digital technologies, can offer a radical new
way of thinking for a more positive way forward that
recognizes the more-than-human connections between
humans, digital data and other living things (Lupton,

2019b). Importantly, such approaches acknowledge the dignity and agency of animals. They elevate animals beyond their objectified, patronized and disempowering 'cute' or 'pet' status, and, in the case of farm animals, their dominant role as a source of food for our consumption or an economic commodity. Instead, these capacious philosophies acknowledge that animals are vibrant, powerful and agential beings that are vital to the ecologies of the more-than-human world. As I argued in chapter 1, the Western world is only just beginning to recognize that when we meddle in the lives, habitats and complex positionings of other animals in place and space, we disrupt the entire ecosystem. First Nations peoples and non-Western cosmologies have always recognized that, rather than humans being positioned as the owners or dominators of other animals, our role should be reoriented as custodians working with animals, other living things, place and space to open shared capacities for action and agency.

The 'Country centred design' approach pioneered by Australian First Nations researchers Angie Abdilla, Megan Kelleher, Rick Shaw and Tyson Yunkaporta (Abdilla et al., 2021) focuses on incorporating the concept of Country (explained in chapter 1) into AI design and software engineering. This approach seeks to include human and nonhuman agents in designing novel technologies, acknowledging that they are inextricably interrelated and that Country, rather than humans, is the centre of these relationships. Humans are positioned as working with digital technologies and the other agents in Country to ensure mutual flourishing. Other First Nations writers have argued for the importance of using Indigenous epistemologies to acknowledge all things as kin, with kinship networks that extend beyond humans and across ecologies: including other animals but also digital technologies. Jason Lewis and colleagues (Lewis et al., 2018) propose 'an extended circle of relationships' that includes 'non-human kin . . . that increasingly populate our computational biosphere'. Building on this concept, they argue that the design of AI technologies should involve creating networks and relationships between technologies, humans and other agents that are reciprocal and respectful, and where humans are not privileged over other agents in these assemblages.

Digital storytelling has been used as a way of providing a voice to First Nations peoples to articulate their ethos of connection, including their relationship with place and the living and non-living occupants who cohabit with humans (Sanchez-Pimienta et al., 2021). An example is an interactive and immersive virtual reality world built by an Australian First Nations digital developer, Kooma man Brett Leavy, and digital tools he has shared to help other First Nations Australians record their songlines (cultural knowledges) and Country. Entitled Virtual Songlines (2022), the software kit is designed to record the First Nations heritage that existed before European invasion and settlement, and to display it in public spaces. Historically significant places and spaces are included in these virtual and augmented-reality simulations to create a digital storytelling experience that enables non-Indigenous viewers to 'walk in the footsteps' of the cultures that are portrayed in an immersive way, bringing together image and sound. Every animal and object portrayed in these virtual stories is programmed so that they react to the humans in ways defined by the traditions of the songlines, bringing to life Australian First Nations knowledges drawn from historical and anthropological research and interviews with elders and other community members. Digital data from other data sets, such as the soil maps generated by

Geoscience Australia, are used together with cultural information about bush medicine, bush foods, hunting grounds, tracks and campsites to reconstruct the real-world biomes that have sustained First Nations peoples and wildlife in Australia over millennia. The plan is to use these virtual worlds for education and cultural heritage purposes and for environmental impact assessments (Hardy, 2020).

Museums, art galleries and science and art exhibitions around the world have begun to experiment with using digital technologies together with more-than-human ways of seeing, doing, thinking and feeling. They have recognized that processes of digitization and datafication can contribute to awakening humans' awareness of the delicate balance of living creatures in local and global ecosystems. One example is the 23rd Biennale of Sydney, 'Rivus', a set of exhibitions at multiple sites in that city which was themed around water: rivers, wetlands and other saltwater and freshwater ecosystems. The artworks encouraged audiences to consider humans' place in the teeming, dynamic and life-giving forms of water within and outside their own bodies. As described by the Museum of Contemporary Art (MCA), one of the sites of the Biennale:

> Rivers are the sediment of culture. They are givers of life, routes of communication, and places of ritual, but also sewers and mass graves. They are witnesses and archives, our memory. They have also been co-opted as natural avenues for the colonial enterprise, becoming sites of violent conflict driven by greed, exploitation, and the thirst to possess. (MCA, 2022)

The Biennale's curatorium directly drew on First Nations' and non-Western perspectives in curating artworks that sought to position nonhuman entities as 'living ancestral beings with a right to life that must be protected' (MCA, 2022). Several artworks involved digital creations which invited audiences to be drawn into the multisensory worlds of creatures who live in or near waterways, asking them to reflect on their relationships with these aqueous beings. 'The Great Animal Orchestra', by American soundscape ecologist Bernie Krause and London-based United Visual Artists, is one example. Held in a tent-like enclosure placed on a grassy lawn at the Cutaway (part of the Barangaroo nature reserve overlooking Sydney Harbour), audiences entered into a dark space that was filled with an immersive soundscape of 15,000 animal species from endangered ecosystems such as tropical grasslands, savannas and the Arctic tundra. Together with light effects, the use of water and movement, this artwork provided insights into 'the unseen world of animals': their complex and multi-layered vocalizations (23rd Biennale of Sydney, 2022).

Other artworks using digital technologies featured in the Biennale were presented by Tabita Rezaire, who lives and works in French Guiana, South America. Rezaire brought together digital images with objects such as standing stones in her video installation 'Mamelles ancestrales'. The work is inspired by African philosophies of the cosmos and the ancient stone circle monuments used in that continent as astronomical tools. In a darkened space within a gallery at the MCA, a flat table-like structure displayed Rezaire's colourful video art, surrounded by the encircling standing stones. Rezaire used this installation to question why settler knowledges relating to science and the environment should be prioritized over the spiritual and cultural insights offered by First Nations philosophies.

The inextricable relational nature of humans' fleshly and affective bonds with the diversity of living things on our planet cannot and should not be denied or rejected any longer if humans and other creatures are to survive and live well long into the future. Together with traditional pre-Enlightenment and contemporary non-Western cosmologies, these viewpoints offer a way forward for developing relational connections between humans, other creatures and living things in the specific places and spaces within which people live and through which they move. Importantly, these perspectives do not seek to generalize about human–animal relationships. Instead, they replace grand narratives with a multitude of diverse situated narratives (Chan, 2018). This focus can help us identify how animal–human–digital assemblages are enacted, including casting light on who (or what) benefits or who (or what) may be harmed. As I have demonstrated in this book, affective intensities and relational connections as they are configured with and through processes of digitization and datafication are not always conducive to human–nonhuman flourishing. While affective forces may impel action and open capacities, these may be harmful or detrimental to humans' and other animals' health and wellbeing. The establishment of relational connections with digital media and devices can exclude other potential connections. We need to think about and practise new forms of interspecies relations that resist human-centric impulses towards control and containment of the irrepressible vibrancies of the rich more-than-human worlds of which we are always a part.

Appendix

The aim of the 'Animals on the Internet' research project was to investigate how people are using digital media and devices to find and share information about animals: including pets, domesticated animals and wild animals. This project involved a short online survey with closed-ended and open-ended questions hosted on the Qualtrics platform. The survey included sociodemographic questions concerning the participant's age, gender and country of residence, followed by questions about pet ownership and whether the participant is vegetarian or vegan, and then questions about the digital media and devices that the participants use to find and share information about animals. These questions were answered by the participants typing in their answers. The project received approval from the University of New South Wales Human Research Ethics Committee.

The survey was shared and publicized using my connections and networks on social media (Twitter and Facebook). It was completed by a total of 130 participants in February–March 2021. The age range of participants was 22 to 76 years. Most of the participants identified as female (84%), with 14% male and

2% providing 'other' as their gender. The majority were resident in the Australia / New Zealand / Pacific region (65%), with a further 13% from the UK, 12% from North America, 8% from Continental Europe and 2% from Asia. The majority of participants (85%) reported that they lived with one or more pets. In an open-ended question, these participants were asked to list their pets: dogs (54%) and cats (38%) were by far the most common, with fish, rabbits, birds (including chickens), goats or sheep, insects and amphibians listed by a further 13% in total, and 1 person each listing pet rats and a horse. A total of 17% of participants listed more than one species as sharing their lives. In terms of dietary choices, 24% reported being vegetarian and 6% vegan.

The remainder of the survey included the following questions:

1 Have you ever used the internet to find information about your pet/s or any other animals? (e.g. websites, discussion forums, blogs, YouTube, Pinterest, social media or message services such as Facebook, Instagram, Snapchat, TikTok or Twitter).

   a. If yes: What have been the most valuable or helpful online sources of information about animals for you?

2 Do you ever upload or share information about your pet/s or any other animals online? (e.g. post images, videos or comments about them on online forums, YouTube, Pinterest or social media or message services such as Facebook, Instagram, Snapchat, TikTok or Twitter).

   a. If yes: Please describe what you do and explain why you do it.

3 Do you use any smartphone apps, wearable devices or any other 'smart' devices to better understand or care for your pet/s or for any other animals?

    a. If yes: Please provide the names of the apps or devices and explain what you find useful or helpful about them.

4 Do you ever look at animal-related content on the internet or apps for entertainment purposes? (e.g. funny or cute animal videos or memes).

    a. If yes: Please describe one recent occasion you have done this, what the content was and where you found it, and what you liked or found valuable about the content.

5 Do you ever look at animal-related content on the internet or apps for dietary, political or activism purposes? (e.g. veganism or animal activism content).

    a. If yes: Please describe one recent occasion you have done this, what the content was and where you found it, and what you liked or found valuable about the content.

6 Do you follow any social media influencers or celebrities who post content online about their pets or about other animals?

    a. If yes: Please provide the names of these people and explain what you like or find interesting about their animal-related content.

7 If you could design a new technology to help you better understand or care for your pet or any other animals – what would it be? Please describe what it would do.

8 Are there any other comments you would like to make about animals and the internet?

References

23rd Biennale of Sydney (2022) The Great Animal Orchestra – Bernie Krause & United Visual Artists. Available at: www.biennaleofsydney.art/participants/the-great-animal-orchestra.

Abdilla A, Kelleher M, Shaw R, et al. (2021) *Out of the Black Box: Indigenous Protocols for AI*. UNESCO.

Abram D (2021) Wild ethics and participatory science: thinking between the body and the breathing earth. In: Van Horn G, Kimmerer RW and Hausdoerffer J (eds.) *Kinship: Belonging in a World of Relations*. Volume 1: *Planet*. Center for Humans & Nature Press, pp. 50–62.

Adams CJ (1990) *The Sexual Politics of Meat: A Feminist-Vegetarian Critical Theory*. Continuum Publishing.

Adams CJ (2010) Why feminist-vegan now? *Feminism & Psychology* 20(3): 302–17.

Adams WM (2017) Geographies of conservation II: technology, surveillance and conservation by algorithm. *Progress in Human Geography* 43(2): 337–50.

Ahmed S (2004) *The Cultural Politics of Emotion*. Edinburgh University Press.

AIST (2022) *Paro Therapeutic Robot*. Available at: www.parorobots.com.

References

Allison A (2004) Cuteness as Japan's millennial product. In: Tobin J (ed.) *Pikachu's Global Adventure: The Rise and Fall of Pokémon.* Duke University Press, pp. 34–49.

Almiron N, Cole M and Freeman CP (2015) *Critical Animal and Media Studies: Communication for Nonhuman Animal Advocacy.* Routledge.

Aloi G (2022) Editorial. *Antennae* Spring: 8–9.

Animal Medicines Australia (2019) *Pets in Australia: A National Survey of Pets and People.* Animal Medicines Australia.

Arcari P (2019) The ethical masquerade: (un)masking mechanisms of power behind 'ethical' meat. In: Phillipov M and Kirkwood K (eds.) *Alternative Food Politics: From the Margins to the Mainstream.* Routledge, pp. 169–89.

Aspling F, Juhlin O and Väätäjä H (2018) Understanding animals: a critical challenge in ACI. In: *Proceedings of the 10th Nordic Conference on Human–Computer Interaction* [Oslo]. ACM, pp. 148–60.

Athanasiadis I (2022) Digital Future Farm. Available at: www.athanasiadis.info/projects/dff.

Baquero OS, Benavidez Fernández MN and Acero Aguilar M (2021) From modern planetary health to decolonial promotion of One Health of Peripheries. *Frontiers in Public Health*, 9. Available at: https://pubmed.ncbi.nlm.nih.gov/34178913.

Barad K (2007) *Meeting the Universe Halfway: Quantum Physics and the Entanglement of Matter and Meaning.* Duke University Press.

Behler A, Green J and Joy-Gaba J (2020) 'We lost a member of the family': predictors of the grief experience surrounding the loss of a pet. *Human Animal Interaction Bulletin* 8(3): 54–70.

Belcourt B-R (2015) Animal bodies, colonial subjects: (re)locating animality in decolonial thought. *Societies* 5. Available at: www.mdpi.com/2075-4698/5/1/1.

Bennett J (2010) A vitalist stopover on the way to a new materialism. In: Coole D and Frost S (eds.) *New Materialisms: Ontology, Agency and Politics.* Duke University Press, pp. 47–69.

Bergman JN, Buxton RT, Lin H-Y, et al. (2022) Evaluating the benefits and risks of social media for wildlife conservation. *FACETS* 7(1): 360–97.

Berland J (2008) Cat and mouse: iconographics of nature and desire. *Cultural Studies* 22(3–4): 431–54.

Blackie S (2021) Kinship and otherness: the fine art of shapeshifting in myth and folklore. In: Van Horn G, Kimmerer RW and Hausdoerffer J (eds.) *Kinship: Belonging in a World of Relations.* Volume 3: *Partners.* Center for Humans & Nature Press, pp. 43–51.

Bos JM, Bovenkerk B, Feindt PH, et al. (2018) The quantified animal: precision livestock farming and the ethical implications of objectification. *Food Ethics* 2(1): 77–92.

Bossert L and Hagendorff T (2021) Animals and AI: the role of animals in AI research and application – an overview and ethical evaluation. *Technology in Society* 67. Available at: www.sciencedirect.com/science/article/pii/S0160791X21001536.

Boston Dynamics (2018) Uptown Spot. Available at: www.youtube.com/watch?v=kHBcVlqpvZ8.

Boston Dynamics (2022) Spot for industrial inspections. Available at: www.bostondynamics.com/solutions/inspection.

Braidotti R (2006) *Transpositions: On Nomadic Ethics.* Polity.

Braidotti R (2016) Posthuman critical theory. In: Banerji D and Paranjape M (eds.) *Critical Posthumanism and Planetary Futures.* Springer, pp. 13–32.

Braun V and Carruthers S (2020) Working at self and wellness: a critical analysis of vegan vlogs. In: Lupton D and Feldman Z (eds.) *Digital Food Cultures*. Routledge, pp. 82–96.

Buddle E (2022) Meet your meat! How Australian livestock producers use Instagram to promote 'happy meat'. In: Contois EJ and Kish Z (eds.) *Food Instagram: Identity, Influence and Negotiation*. University of Illinois Press, pp. 163–76.

BuzzBingo (2022) Pet TikTok Richlist 2021. Available at: www.buzzbingo.com/bingo-games/tik-tok-pets.

Campbell DLM, Ouzman J, Mowat D, et al. (2020) Virtual fencing technology excludes beef cattle from an environmentally sensitive area. *Animals* 10. Available at: www.mdpi.com/2076-2615/10/6/1069/htm.

Caudwell C and Lacey C (2020) What do home robots want? The ambivalent power of cuteness in robotic relationships. *Convergence* 26(4): 956–68.

Chan TM (2018) Postanimalism. In: Braidotti R and Hlavajova M (eds.) *Posthuman Glossary*. Bloomsbury Academic, pp. 329–32.

Chiew F (2014) Posthuman ethics with Cary Wolfe and Karen Barad: animal compassion as trans-species entanglement. *Theory, Culture & Society* 31(4): 51–69.

Coeckelbergh M (2011) Humans, animals, and robots: a phenomenological approach to human–robot relations. *International Journal of Social Robotics* 3(2): 197–204.

Coghlan S, Coghlan BJ, Capon A, et al. (2021) A bolder One Health: expanding the moral circle to optimize health for all. *One Health Outlook* 3. Available at: https://doi.org/10.1186/s42522-021-00053-8.

Coghlan S and Sparrow L (2021) The 'digital animal intuition': the ethics of violence against animals in video games. *Ethics and Information Technology* 23(3): 215–24.

Cole M and Stewart K (2017) 'A new life in the countryside awaits': interactive lessons in the rural utopia in 'farming' simulation games. *Discourse: Studies in the Cultural Politics of Education* 38(3): 402–15.

Collard R-C (2016) Electric elephants and the lively/lethal energies of wildlife documentary film. *Area* 48(4): 472–9.

Conard K (2021) The origins of the Grumpy Cat meme. *The List*. Available at: www.thelist.com/587482/the-ori gins-of-the-grumpy-cat-meme.

Cornell Lab of Ornithology (2022) *eBird*. Available at:. https://ebird.org/home.

Cudworth E (2015) Killing animals: sociology, species relations and institutionalized violence. *The Sociological Review* 63(1): 1–18.

Curry A (2018) The internet of animals that could help to save vanishing wildlife. *Nature.com*. Available at: www .nature.com/articles/d41586-018-07036-2.

Dale JP, Goggin J, Leyda J, et al. (2017) The aesthetics and affects of cuteness. In: Dale JP, Goggin J, Leyda J, et al. (eds.) *The Aesthetics and Affects of Cuteness*. Routledge, pp. 1–34.

Delfanti A (2021) Machinic dispossession and augmented despotism: digital work in an Amazon warehouse. *New Media & Society* 23(1): 39–55.

DeMello M (2021) *Animals and Society: An Introduction to Human–Animal Studies*. Columbia University Press.

Dobson AS, Robards B and Carah N (2018) *Digital Intimate Publics and Social Media*. Palgrave Macmillan.

DogStar (2022) TailTalk 'world's first dog emotion sensor'. *DogStar Life*. Available at: www.dogstar.life/tailtalk-1.

Dorward LJ, Mittermeier JC, Sandbrook C, et al. (2017) Pokémon Go: benefits, costs, and lessons for the conservation movement. *Conservation Letters* 10(1): 160–5.

Douglas M (1966) *Purity and Danger: An Analysis of Concepts of Pollution and Taboo*. Routledge & Kegan Paul.

References

Douglas M (1992) *Risk and Blame: Essays in Cultural Theory.* Routledge.

Edwards-Murphy F, Magno M, Whelan PM, et al. (2016) b+WSN: smart beehive with preliminary decision tree analysis for agriculture and honey bee health monitoring. *Computers and Electronics in Agriculture* 124: 211–19.

Elias N (1978) *The Civilizing Process.* Urizen.

Elish MC and boyd d (2018) Situating methods in the magic of Big Data and AI. *Communication Monographs* 85(1): 57–80.

Emmanouil O (2021) Listening to a river's law. In: Van Horn G, Kimmerer RW and Hausdoerffer J (eds.) *Kinship: Belonging in a World of Relations.* Volume 3: *Partners.* Center for Humans & Nature Press, pp. 24–34.

Enabot (2022) Available at: https://na.enabot.com.

Equilinox.com (2022) Available at: https://equilinox.com.

Evans NJ and Moore AR (2019) Is there a turtle in this text? Animals in the Internet of Robots and Things. *Animal Studies Journal* 8(1): 21–41.

Faheid D (2021) The newest TikTok stars are exotic pets, but experts say that's a problem. *NPR.* Available at: www.npr.org/2021/07/04/1012502556/tiktok-exotic-pets-videos-responsibility-of-ownership.

Feber RE, Raebel EM, D'cruze N, et al. (2017) Some animals are more equal than others: wild animal welfare in the media. *Bioscience* 67(1): 62–72.

Feral Atlas (2021) *Feral Atlas: The More-than-Human Anthropocene.* Available at: http://feralatlas.org.

Finch J (2020) Why 'Animal Crossing: New Horizons' became a cultural phenomenon. *How-to-Geek.* Available at: www.howtogeek.com/671064/why-animal-crossing-new-horizons-became-a-cultural-phenomenon.

Fink S (2021) From climate change to culls, threats against

harp seals continue in 2021. *IFAW*. Available at: www
.ifaw.org/journal/climate-change-threats-seals.

Fitbark.com (2022) Available at: www.fitbark.com.

Fothergill B and Flick C (2016) The ethics of human–
chicken relationships in video games: the origins of the
digital chicken. *ACM SIGCAS Computers and Society*
45(3): 100–8.

Fox R and Gee NR (2019) Great expectations: changing
social, spatial and emotional understandings of the companion animal–human relationship. *Social & Cultural
Geography* 20(1): 43–63.

Frazzoli C, Ruggieri F, Battistini B, et al. (2022) E-waste
threatens health: the scientific solution adopts the
One Health strategy. *Environmental Research* 212.
Available at: www.sciencedirect.com/science/article/pii/
S0013935122005540.

Frichot H (2022) Scarred trees and becoming-witness.
Angelaki 27(2): 114–29.

Gaard G (2015) Ecofeminism and climate change. *Women's
Studies International Forum* 49: 20–33.

Gabrys J (2019) Sensors and sensing practices: reworking
experience across entities, environments, and technologies. *Science, Technology, & Human Values* 44(5):
723–36.

Gabulaitė V (2016) 77 celebrity doppelganger animals.
Bored Panda. Available at: www.boredpanda.com/celeb
rity-look-alikes-animals/?utm_source=google&utm_me
dium=organic&utm_campaign=organic.

Gellers JC (2021) *Rights for Robots: Artificial Intelligence, Animal and Environmental Law (Edition 1)*.
Routledge.

Goifetch.com (2022) Available at: https://store.skymee
.com.

Greenhough B, Read CJ, Lorimer J, et al. (2020) Setting
the agenda for social science research on the human

microbiome. *Palgrave Communications* 6. Available at: https://doi.org/10.1057/s41599-020-0388-5.

Grosz E (1994) *Volatile Bodies: Toward a Corporeal Feminism*. Allen & Unwin.

Hagendorff T, Bossert L, Fai TY, et al. (2022) Speciesist bias in AI: how AI applications perpetuate discrimination and unfair outcomes against animals. *arXiv*. Available at: https://arxiv.org/abs/2202.10848v1.

Haraway D (1985) Manifesto for cyborgs: science, technology, and socialist feminism in the 1980s. *Socialist Review* 80: 65–108.

Haraway D (1988) Situated knowledges: the science question in feminism and the privilege of partial perspective. *Feminist Studies* 14(3): 575–99.

Haraway D (2003) *The Companion Species Manifesto: Dogs, People, and Significant Otherness*. Prickly Paradigm.

Haraway D (2015) Birth of the kennel: a lecture by Donna Haraway, August 2000. *The European Graduate School*. Available at: www.egs.edu/faculty/donna-haraway/artic les/birth-of-the-kennel.

Haraway D (2016) *Staying with the Trouble: Making Kin in the Chthulucene*. Duke University Press.

Haraway D and Goodeve TNG (2000) *How Like a Leaf: An Interview with Thyrza Nicols Goodeve*. Routledge.

Hardey M (2022) *Household Self-Tracking during a Global Health Crisis: Shaping Bodies, Lives, Health and Illness*. Emerald.

Hardy E (2020) This Indigenous creator built a virtual reality program to celebrate First Nations cultures. *Create*. Available at: https://createdigital.org.au/indigenous-crea tor-builds-virtual-reality-program-first-nations-cultures.

Hartnell J (2018) *Medieval Bodies: Life, Death and Art in the Middle Ages*. Profile Books.

Helgason T, Daniell T, Husband R, et al. (1998) Ploughing up the wood-wide web? *Nature* 394(6692): 431.

Hernández KJ, Rubis JM, Theriault N, et al. (2020) The Creatures Collective: manifestings. *Environment and Planning E: Nature and Space* 4(3): 838–63.

Hibberd J (2017) *Black Mirror* creator explains that 'Metalhead' robot nightmare. *Entertainment Weekly*. Available at: https://ew.com/tv/2017/12/29/black-mirror-metalhead-interview.

Hill S (2021) Games rule the app stores: most popular genres 2020–2021. *Localize Direct*. Available at: www.localizedirect.com/posts/most-popular-game-genres-revealed.

Hinchliffe S (2022) Postcolonial global health, post-colony microbes and antimicrobial resistance. *Theory, Culture & Society* 39(3): 145–68.

Hjorth L and Lupton D (2021) Digitised caring intimacies: more-than-human intergenerational care in Japan. *International Journal of Cultural Studies* 24(4): 584–602.

Holloway L and Bear C (2017) Bovine and human becomings in histories of dairy technologies: robotic milking systems and remaking animal and human subjectivity. *BJHS Themes* 2: 215–34.

Hong S-H (2015) When life mattered: the politics of the real in video games' reappropriation of history, myth, and ritual. *Games and Culture* 10(1): 35–56.

Hudson-Smith A, Hay D, Wilson D, et al. (2019) *The Little Book of Connected Environments and the Internet of Things*. ImaginationLancaster.

I Can Haz Cheezburger? (2022a) *I Can Haz Cheezburger?* Available at: https://icanhas.cheezburger.com.

I Can Haz Cheezburger? (2022b) Time to take in the weekly dose of cute cats (#183). *I Can Haz Cheezburger?*

Available at: https://cheezburger.com/1696128 5/time-to
-take-in-the-weekly-dose-of-cute-cats-183.

ICARUS (2022) The internet of animals. Available at:
www.icarus.mpg.de/28056/about-icarus.

IFAW (2022) About IFAW. *IFAW*. Available at: www
.ifaw.org/about.

ilume.com (2022) Available at: www.weareilume.com/
how-it-works.

Irni K (2020) Queering multispecies bonding: read-
ing Donna Haraway's dog stories as queer feminism.
Humanimalia 12(1): 188–209.

Iyer V (2022) Living IoT. Available at: http://livingiot.cs
.washington.edu/#abstract.

Iyer V, Nandakumar R, Wang A, et al. (2019) Living IoT:
a flying wireless platform on live insects. In: *Proceedings
of the 25th Annual International Conference on Mobile
Computing and Networking* [Los Carbos]. ACM.
Available at: https://dl.acm.org/doi/10.1145/3300061
.3300136.

Jasanoff S (2015) Future imperfect: science, technology, and
the imaginations of modernity. In: Jasanoff S and Kim
S-H (eds.) *Dreamscapes of Modernity: Sociotechnical
Imaginaries and the Fabrication of Power*. University of
Chicago Press, pp. 1–33.

Jensen CB and Blok A (2013) Techno-animism in Japan:
Shinto cosmograms, actor-network theory, and the ena-
bling powers of non-human agencies. *Theory, Culture
& Society* 30(2): 84–115.

John N (2017) *The Age of Sharing*. Polity.

Kagan S (2018) For hierarchy in animal ethics. *Journal of
Practical Ethics* 6. Available at: https://papers.ssrn.com/
sol3/papers.cfm?abstract_id=3202735.

Kalte D (2021) Political veganism: an empirical analysis of vegans' motives, aims, and political engagement.
Political Studies 69(4): 814–33.

References

Kanesaka E (2022) The healing power of virtual cuteness. *Public Books*. Available at: www.publicbooks.org/kawa ii-cuteness-in-animal-crossing-new-horizons.

Karthick GS, Sridhar M and Pankajavalli PB (2020) Internet of Things in animal healthcare (IoTAH): review of recent advancements in architecture, sensing technologies and real-time monitoring. *SN Computer Science* 1. Available at: https://doi.org/10.1007/s42979-020-00 310-z.

Klauser F (2018) Surveillance farm: towards a research agenda on big data agriculture. *Surveillance & Society* 16(3): 370–8.

Klerkx L, Jakku E and Labarthe P (2019) A review of social science on digital agriculture, smart farming and agriculture 4.0: new contributions and a future research agenda. *NJAS-Wageningen Journal of Life Sciences* 90. Available at: www.sciencedirect.com/science/article/pii/ S1573521419301769.

Knezevic I, Pasho J and Dobson K (2018) Seal hunts in Canada and on Twitter: exploring the tensions between Indigenous rights and animal rights with #Sealfie. *Canadian Journal of Communication* 43(3): 421–39.

Know Your Meme (2022) Grumpy Cat. Available at: https://knowyourmeme.com/memes/grumpy-cat.

Kogan LR, Little S and Oxley J (2021) Dog and cat owners' use of online Facebook groups for pet health information. *Health Information & Libraries Journal* 38(3): 203–23.

Krause-Parello CA, Gulick EE and Basin B (2019) Loneliness, depression, and physical activity in older adults: the therapeutic role of human–animal interactions. *Anthrozoös* 32(2): 239–54.

Kristeva J (1982) *Powers of Horror: An Essay on Abjection.* Columbia University Press.

Kuoljok K (2019) Without land we are lost: traditional

knowledge, digital technology and power relations. *AlterNative: An International Journal of Indigenous Peoples* 15(4): 349–58.

Laforteza EM (2014) Cute-ifying disability: Lil bub, the celebrity cat. *M/C Journal* 17. Available at: http://jour nal.media-culture.org.au/index.php/mcjournal/article/vi ew/784.

Lee C, Colditz IG and Campbell DL (2018) A framework to assess the impact of new animal management technologies on welfare: a case study of virtual fencing. *Frontiers in Veterinary Science* 5. Available at: www.fr ontiersin.org/articles/10.3389/fvets.2018.00187/full.

Leijser B (2022) Games that reward you for being vegetarian or vegan. *The Gamer*. Available at: www.thegamer .com/games-that-reward-you-for-being-vegetarian.

Lely.com (2022) The new milestone in cow comfort. Available at: www.lely.com/au/solutions/milking/astro naut-a5/cow-comfort.

Lewis JE, Arista N, Pechawis A, et al. (2018) Making kin with the machines. *Journal of Design and Science* 3. Available at: https://jods.mitpress.mit.edu/pub/lewis-aris ta-pechawis-kite/release/1?platform=hootsuite.

lilbub.com (2022) Available at: https://lilbub.com.

Linné T (2016) Cows on Facebook and Instagram: interspecies intimacy in the social media spaces of the Swedish dairy industry. *Television & New Media* 17(8): 719–33.

Linzey A and Linzey C (2018) Introduction: the challenge of animal ethics. In: Linzey A and Linzey C (eds.) *The Palgrave Handbook of Practical Animal Ethics*. Palgrave Macmillan, pp. 1–22.

Lockie S, Fairley-Grenot K, Ankeny R, et al. (2020) *The Future of Agricultural Technologies*. Australian Council of Learned Academies.

Lupton D (1995) The embodied computer/user. *Body & Society* 1(3–4): 97–112.

Lupton D (1996) *Food, the Body and the Self.* Sage.

Lupton D (2015) *Digital Sociology.* Routledge.

Lupton D (2016) *The Quantified Self: A Sociology of Self-Tracking.* Polity.

Lupton D (2017) *Digital Health: Critical and Cross-Disciplinary Perspectives.* Routledge.

Lupton D (2018) Cooking, eating, uploading: digital food cultures. In: LeBesco K and Naccarato P (eds.) *The Handbook of Food and Popular Culture.* Bloomsbury, pp. 66–79.

Lupton D (2019a) Caring dataveillance: women's use of apps to monitor pregnancy and children. In: Green L, Holloway D, Stevenson K, et al. (eds.) *The Routledge Companion to Digital Media and Children.* Routledge, pp. 393–402.

Lupton D (2019b) *Data Selves: More-than-Human Perspectives.* Polity.

Lupton D (2019c) Toward a more-than-human analysis of digital health: inspirations from feminist new materialism. *Qualitative Health Research* 29(14): 1998–2006.

Lupton D (2019d) Vitalities and visceralities: alternative body/food politics in new digital media. In: Phillipov M and Kirkwood K (eds.) *Alternative Food Politics: From the Margins to the Mainstream.* Routledge, pp. 151–68.

Lupton D (2020a) Carnivalesque food videos: excess, gender and affect on YouTube. In: Lupton D and Feldman Z (eds.) *Digital Food Cultures.* Routledge, pp. 35–49.

Lupton D (2020b) The Internet of Things: social dimensions. *Sociology Compass* 14(4). Available at: https://compass.onlinelibrary.wiley.com/doi/abs/10.1111/soc4.12770.

Lupton D (2020c) A more-than-human approach to bioethics: the example of digital health. *Bioethics* 34(9): 969–76.

References

Lupton D (2021) Language matters: the 'digital twin' metaphor in health and medicine. *Journal of Medical Ethics* 47(6): 409.

Lupton D (2022) *COVID Societies: Theorising the Coronavirus Crisis*. Routledge.

Lupton D, Clark M and Southerton C (2022) Digitized and datafied embodiment: a more-than-human approach. In: Herbrechter S, Callus I, Rossini M, et al. (eds.) *Palgrave Handbook of Critical Posthumanism*. Springer International Publishing. Available at: https://doi.org/10.1007/978-3-030-42681-1_65-1.

Lupton D and Lewis S (2022) Coping with COVID-19: the sociomaterial dimensions of living with pre-existing mental illness during the early stages of the coronavirus crisis. *Emotion, Space and Society* 42. Available at: www.sciencedirect.com/science/article/pii/S1755458621000980.

Lupton D and Williamson B (2017) The datafied child: the dataveillance of children and implications for their rights. *New Media & Society* 19(5): 780–94.

Lyon D (2018) *The Culture of Surveillance: Watching as a Way of Life*. John Wiley & Sons.

MacNeil J (2014) Inuit singer Tanya Tagaq's 'selfie' photo supporting seal hunt sparks backlash. *HuffPost*. Available at: www.huffpost.com/archive/ca/entry/inuit-tanya-tagaq-sealfie_n_5077203.

Maddox J (2021) The secret life of pet Instagram accounts: joy, resistance, and commodification in the Internet's cute economy. *New Media & Society* 23(11): 3332–48.

Malamud R (2012) *An Introduction to Animals and Visual Culture*. Palgrave Macmillan.

MammalWeb (2022) *MammalWeb*. Available at: www.mammalweb.org/en/#.

Manning J, Power D and Cosby A (2021) Legal complexities of animal welfare in Australia: do on-animal sensors offer a future option? *Animals* 11. Available at: www .mdpi.com/2076-2615/11/1/91.

Maras M-H and Wandt AS (2019) Enabling mass surveillance: data aggregation in the age of big data and the Internet of Things. *Journal of Cyber Policy* 4(2): 160–77.

Mather JA (2019) Ethics and care: for animals, not just mammals. *Animals* 9. Available at: www.mdpi.com/20 76-2615/9/12/1018.

May S (2019) *The Power of Cute.* Princeton University Press.

Mbembe A (2019) *Necropolitics.* Duke University Press.

MCA (2022) 23rd Biennale of Sydney: Rivus. Available at: www.mca.com.au/artists-works/exhibitions/23rd-bien nale-of-sydney-rivus/?gclid=CjwKCAjwx46TBhBhEiwA rA_DjB7XAsX4lcGW3iSPzp1KHA7pcIU1gfY2jx_ju wOm_PWyYeaxIHbpkxoCxO8QAvD_BwE.

McCance D (2012) *Critical Animal Studies: An Introduction.* SUNY Press.

McCurry J (2018) Japan: robot dogs get solemn Buddhist send-off at funerals. *The Guardian.* Available at: www .theguardian.com/world/2018/may/03/japan-robot-dogs -get-solemn-buddhist-send-off-at-funerals.

McParlan J and van der Linden D (2021) Privacy labels should go to the dogs. In: *Proceedings of Eighth International Conference on Animal–Computer Interaction* [Bloomington]. ACM, pp. 1–10. Available at: https://dl.acm.org/doi/10.1145/3493842.3493888.

Meese J (2014) 'It belongs to the internet': animal images, attribution norms and the politics of amateur media production. *M/C Journal* 17. Available at: https://journal .media-culture.org.au/index.php/mcjournal/article/view /782.

Mills B (2010) Television wildlife documentaries and animals' right to privacy. *Continuum* 24(2): 193–202.

Mills B (2017) *Animals on Television: The Cultural Making of the Non-Human.* Springer.

Mokal B and Sharma A (2020) Use cases: digital twin in livestock farming. *Aranca.* Available at: www.aranca .com/knowledge-library/articles/ip-research/use-cases-di gital-twin-in-livestock-farming#:~:text=Digital%20twin %20technology%20can%20help,%2C%20SARS%2C %20Ebola%20and%20Coronavirus.

Molloy C (2011) *Popular Media and Animals.* Palgrave Macmillan.

Mori M (1970/2012) The uncanny valley: the original essay by Masahiro Mori. *IEEE Robots & Automation Magazine* June. Available at: https://ieeexplore.ieee.org/ stamp/stamp.jsp?arnumber=6213238.

Mowbray S (2022) Facial recognition – now for seals. *Hakai Magazine.* Available at: https://hakaimagazine .com/news/facial-recognition-now-for-seals.

Mukherjee S and Lundedal Hammar E (2018) Introduction to the special issue on postcolonial perspectives in game studies. *Open Library of Humanities* 4. Available at: https://olh.openlibhums.org/article/id/4527.

Murphy F, Magno M, O' Leary L, et al. (2015) Big brother for bees (3B) – energy neutral platform for remote monitoring of beehive imagery and sound. In: *Proceedings of the 2015 6th International Workshop on Advances in Sensors and Interfaces* [Gallipoli, Italy]. IEEE, pp. 106–11.

Murray A (2020) Coronavirus: Denmark shaken by cull of millions of mink. *BBC News.* Available at: www.bbc .com/news/world-europe-54890229.

Murray S (2017) *On Video Games: The Visual Politics of Race, Gender and Space.* Bloomsbury Publishing.

Mwangi W, de Figueiredo P and Criscitiello MF (2016) One Health: addressing global challenges at the nexus of human, animal, and environmental health. *PLOS*

References

Pathogens 12. Available at: https://doi.org/10.1371/jour nal.ppat.1005731.

Nagy P and Neff G (2015) Imagined affordance: reconstructing a keyword for communication theory. *Social Media + Society* 1. Available at: http://sms.sagepub.com/content/1/2/2056305115603385.abstractN2.

Ngai S (2005) The cuteness of the avant-garde. *Critical Inquiry* 31(4): 811–47.

Niloofar P, Francis DP, Lazarova-Molnar S, et al. (2021) Data-driven decision support in livestock farming for improved animal health, welfare and greenhouse gas emissions: overview and challenges. *Computers and Electronics in Agriculture* 190. Available at: www.sciencedirect.com/science/article/pii/S0168169921004233.

Nittono H, Lieber-Milo S and Dale JP (2021) Cross-cultural comparisons of the cute and related concepts in Japan, the United States, and Israel. *SAGE Open* 11. Available at: https://journals.sagepub.com/doi/full/10.1177/21582440020988730.

Noik S (2017) Your wildlife selfies are hurting the animals. *CBC*. Available at: www.cbc.ca/news/science/wildlife-selfies-good-and-bad-1.4340944.

Nunn G (2021) 'They're territorial': can birds and drones coexist? *The Guardian*. Available at: www.theguardian.com/environment/2021/oct/01/theyre-territorial-can-birds-and-drones-coexist.

O D (2021) 30 animal TikToks we can't get enough of. *Little Things*. Available at: https://littlethings.com/pets/funny-animal-tiktoks.

OECD (2016) The Internet of Things: seizing the benefits and addressing the challenges. *OECD Digital Economy Papers*. Available at: www.oecd-ilibrary.org/science-and-technology/the-internet-of-things_5jlwvzz8tdon-en.

O'Meara R (2014) Do cats know they rule YouTube?

Surveillance and the pleasures of cat videos. *M/C Journal* 17. Available at: https://journal.media-culture.org.au/index.php/mcjournal/article/view/794.

O'Neill R (2022) Assassin's Creed Valhalla: all of the animals who can join you on your adventures (and how to get them). *The Gamer*. Available at: www.thegamer.com/assassins-creed-valhalla-animal-companions.

O'Rourke A (1998) Caring about virtual pets: an ethical interpretation of Tamagotchi. *Animal Issues* 2(1): 1.

Packer R, Brand CL, Belshaw Z, et al. (2021) Pandemic puppies: characterising motivations and behaviours of UK owners who purchased puppies during the 2020 COVID-19 pandemic. *Animals* 11. Available at: www.mdpi.com/2076-2615/11/9/2500.

Packer RM (2021) Flat-faced fandom: why do people love brachycephalic dogs and keep coming back for more? In: Packer RM and O'Neill DG (eds.) *Health and Welfare of Brachycephalic (Flat-Faced) Animal Companions*. CRC Press, pp. 25–40.

Page A (2016) 'This baby sloth will inspire you to keep going': capital, labor, and the affective power of cute animal videos. In: Dale JP, Goggin J, Leyda J, et al. (eds.) *The Aesthetics and Affects of Cuteness*. Routledge, pp. 85–104.

Parkinson C (2019) *Animals, Anthropomorphism and Mediated Encounters*. Routledge.

PETA (2022a) *PETA*. Available at: www.peta.org.

PETA (2022b) *PETA's Games*. Available at: www.peta.org/features/games.

Petcube.com (2022) Available at: https://petcube.com.

Plumwood V (2002) *Feminism and the Mastery of Nature*. Routledge.

Puac S (2022) 22 fascinating pet industry statistics and facts (2022 update). *Petpedia*. Available at: https://petpedia.co/pet-industry-statistics.

Qoobo (2022) *What's Qoobo*. Available at: https://qoo bo.info/index-en.

Rainforest Connection (2022) Available at: https://rfcx.org /our_work.

Riley M and Robertson B (2021) #farming365 – exploring farmers' social media use and the (re)presentation of farming lives. *Journal of Rural Studies* 87: 99–111.

Riley S (2022) *The Commodification of Farm Animals*. Springer International Publishing.

Robinson JM, Harrison PA, Mavoa S, et al. (2022) Existing and emerging uses of drones in restoration ecology. *Methods in Ecology and Evolution*, online first. Available at: https://besjournals.onlinelibrary.wiley.com /doi/abs/10.1111/2041-210X.13912.

Robinson M (2014) Animal personhood in Mi'kmaq perspective. *Societies* 4(4): 672–88.

Rodak O (2020) Hashtag hijacking and crowdsourcing transparency: social media affordances and the governance of farm animal protection. *Agriculture and Human Values* 37(2): 281–94.

Rots AP (2017) *Shinto, Nature and Ideology in Contemporary Japan: Making Sacred Forests*. Bloomsbury Publishing.

Roy EA (2019) It's scary: wildlife selfies harming animals, experts warn. *The Guardian*. Available at: www.thegu ardian.com/environment/2019/sep/03/its-scary-wildlife -selfies-harming-animals-experts-warn.

Rutkin A (2014) Sensor backpacks for oysters say when they are happy. *New Scientist*. Available at: www.news cientist.com/article/mg22129584-500-sensor-backpacks -for-oysters-say-when-they-are-happy.

Sanchez-Pimienta CE, Masuda J and M'Wikwedong Indigenous Friendship Centre (2021) From controlling to connecting: M'Wikwedong as a place of urban

Indigenous health promotion in Canada. *Health Promotion International* 36(3): 703–13.

Schellin H, Oberley T, Patterson K, et al. (2020) Man's new best friend? Strengthening human–robot dog bonding by enhancing the doglikeness of Sony's Aibo. In: *Proceedings of the 2020 Systems and Information Engineering Design Symposium (SIEDS)* [Charlottesville]. IEEE.

Sheldrake M (2020) *Entangled Life: How Fungi Make Our Worlds, Change Our Minds & Shape Our Futures.* Random House.

Shildrick M (1997) *Leaky Bodies and Boundaries: Feminism, Postmodernism and (Bio)ethics.* Routledge.

Singer P (1975) *Animal Liberation.* Random House.

Skymee.com (2022) Available at: https://store.skymee.com.

Smith V (2020) 9 vegan YouTubers you need to watch! *Vegan Food and Living.* Available at: www.veganfoodandliving.com/vegan-lifestyle/vegan-youtubers-you-need-to-watch.

Srivastava M and Psaros M (2022) Internet of Elephants: using AR to build a herd of urban conservationists. *Unity.* Available at: https://blog.unity.com/community/internet-of-elephants-using-ar-to-build-a-herd-of-urban-conservationists.

Statista (2020) Most-followed pets on Instagram worldwide as of June 2020. Available at: www.statista.com/statistics/785972/most-followers-instagram-petfluencers.

Statista (2022) Share of households owning a pet in the United Kingdom (UK) from 2011/12 to 2021/22. *Statista.* Available at: www.statista.com/statistics/308235/estimated-pet-ownership-in-the-united-kingdom-uk.

Stojanovic M (2022a) More owners use internet to find new products since COVID-19. *Petpedia.* Available at: https://petpedia.co/news-more-owners-use-internet-to-find-new-products-since-covid-19.

References

Stojanovic M (2022b) Pet industry reaches $123 billion in sales. *Petpedia*. Available at: https://petpedia.co/news-pet-industry-reaches-123-billion-in-sales.

Strengers Y, Kennedy J, Arcari P, et al. (2019a) Protection, productivity and pleasure in the smart home: emerging expectations and gendered insights from Australian early adopters. In: *Proceedings of the 2019 CHI Conference on Human Factors in Computing Systems* [Glasgow]. ACM. Available at: https://dl.acm.org/doi/10.1145/329 0605.3300875.

Strengers Y, Pink S and Nicholls L (2019b) Smart energy futures and social practice imaginaries: forecasting scenarios for pet care in Australian homes. *Energy Research & Social Science* 48: 108–15.

TallBear K (2015) An indigenous reflection on working beyond the human/not human. *GLQ: A Journal of Lesbian and Gay Studies* 21(2–3): 230–5.

Taylor A and Taylor S (2020) Solidarity across species. *Dissent* 67(3): 103–5.

Taylor C (1989) *Sources of the Self: The Making of Modern Identity*. Cambridge University Press.

Taylor N and Sutton Z (2018) For an emancipatory animal sociology. *Journal of Sociology* 54(4): 467–87.

Taylor N and Twine R (2014) *The Rise of Critical Animal Studies: From the Margins to the Centre*. Routledge.

Tester K (1991) *Animals and Society: The Humanity of Animal Rights*. Routledge.

Thomas S (2013) *Technobiophilia: Nature and Cyberspace*. Bloomsbury.

ToadScan (2022) *What ToadScan Provides*. Available at: www.feralscan.org.au/toadscan/pagecontent.aspx?page=toad_whattoadscanprovides.

Todd Z (2016) An Indigenous feminist's take on the ontological turn: 'ontology' is just another word for colonialism. *Journal of Historical Sociology* 29(1): 4–22.

Tombot (2022) Available at: https://tombot.com.

Tronto JC (1993) *Moral Boundaries: A Political Argument for an Ethic of Care*. Routledge.

Tsing AL (2015) *The Mushroom at the End of the World: On the Possibility of Life in Capitalist Ruins*. Princeton University Press.

Tynan L (2021) What is relationality? Indigenous knowledges, practices and responsibilities with kin. *cultural geographies* 28(4): 597–610.

van Dijck J (2014) Datafication, dataism and dataveillance: Big Data between scientific paradigm and ideology. *Surveillance & Society* 12(2): 197–208.

Van Dooren T, Kirksey E and Münster U (2016) Multispecies studies: cultivating arts of attentiveness. *Journal of Environmental Humanities* 8(1): 1–23.

van Ooijen E (2018) On the brink of virtual extinction: hunting and killing animals in open world video games. *Eludamos: Journal for Computer Game Culture* 9(1): 33–45.

Vegan Outreach (2022) *Vegan Outreach*. Available at: https://veganoutreach.org.

Virtual Songlines (2022) *About Us*. Available at: www.virtualsonglines.org/about.

von Essen E, Turnbull J, Searle A, et al. (2021) Wildlife in the digital Anthropocene: examining human–animal relations through surveillance technologies. *Environment and Planning E: Nature and Space*, online first. Available at: https://doi.org/10.1177/25148486211061704.

Weik T (2020) Japanese cultural references you may not have noticed in Animal Crossing: New Horizons. *Yo! Magazine*. Available at: www.itsyozine.com/posts/animal-crossing.

Weingarten R (2021) Aww! The 25 best animal live

cams to watch to see animal babies this spring. *Parade*. Available at: https://parade.com/1015445/rachelweingarten/best-animal-live-cams.

WePC (2022) Video game industry statistics, trends and data in 2022. *WePC*. Available at: www.wepc.com/news/video-game-statistics.

Whistle.com (2022) Available at: www.whistle.com.

White D and Katsuno H (2021) Toward an affective sense of life: artificial intelligence, animacy, and amusement at a robot pet memorial service in Japan. *Cultural Anthropology* 36(2): 222–51.

Wildeverse (2022) *Wildeverse*. Available at: www.wildeversegame.com.

Wolf M (2015) Is there really such a thing as 'one health'? Thinking about a more than human world from the perspective of cultural anthropology. *Social Science & Medicine* 129: 5–11.

Wolfe C (2010) *What Is Posthumanism?* University of Minnesota Press.

Wonneberger A, Hellsten IR and Jacobs SH (2021) Hashtag activism and the configuration of counterpublics: Dutch animal welfare debates on Twitter. *Information, Communication & Society* 24(12): 1694–711.

Woollaston V (2015) Is it cruel to kick a robotic dog? Google video reignites debate over whether machines should be treated like living animals. *Daily Mail Australia*. Available at: www.dailymail.co.uk/sciencetech/article-2955544/Would-kick-robotic-dog-Google-video-regnites-debate-machines-treated-like-living-animals.html.

Wyatt T, Miralles O, Massé F, et al. (2022) Wildlife trafficking via social media in Brazil. *Biological Conservation* 265. Available at: www.sciencedirect.com/science/article/pii/S0006320721004729.

Index

Index

Index

Buddhism
  Buddhist funerals for
    zoomorphic robots
    145
  and Japanese gaming 131
BuzzBingo, 'Pet TikTok Rich
  List' 55

cameras
  CCTV cameras 84
  monitoring pets 93
Canada, seal hunting 68–73
capitalism
  and animal cuteness and
    celebrity cultures
    119–20
  and more-than-human
    perspectives 47
captivity, animals in 3
care
  between humans and
    animals 162
  and dataveillance 79,
    91–7, 98–100,
    158–9
  imagined new technologies
    for caring for animals
    154–5
  power relations involved
    in 120–7
  queering relations of care
    50, 161
cats 3
  anthropomorphizing of
    10, 11
  'Cats Being Weird Little
    Guys' 1–2

and cuteness on social
  media 103–5, 115
and dataveillance 93, 94,
  154
Grumpy Cat 14, 109–10,
  111, 112, 122
internet advice for owners
  8
Lil BUB 110–11, 112,
  122
Nala Cat 112
translators 155
CCTV cameras 84
celebrities, and animal
  activism 61
celebrity cultures 25, 101–2,
  109–14
'celebrity doppelganger
  animals' 113–14
dark side of 118–27
Grumpy Cat 14, 109–10,
  111, 112, 122
Lil BUB 110–11, 112
and selfies with wild
  animals 124–5
Chan, Tsz Man 50, 161,
  163
charismatic species of
  animals, and
  conservation 75
Cheezburger 105
chickens, in computer games
  135–6
China 16
circuses 76
citizen science 53–6, 100,
  126

Index

dogs
  anthropomorphizing of
    10, 11
  as companion species 44
  and cuteness culture 105
  dangerous 16
  dataveillance of 91–6,
    100, 154
  Doug the Pug 112,
    122–3
  Jiff Pomm 111–12
  Mishka the Talking Husky
    114
  and online cuteness
    cultures 106–7, 108
  owners and internet advice
    8
  translators 155
  zoomorphic robots
    Aibo 144–6, 147, 151
    Boston Dynamics,
      'Spot' 147–8,
      149–50, 151
    Jennie robot puppy 51,
      142–3
    and the 'uncanine
      valley' 151–2
DogStar company 95
Doug the Pug 112, 122–3
Douglas, Mary 27
drones 6, 81, 84, 89, 158
Durham University / Wildlife
  Trust 54

Ebo (AI companion robot)
  93
ecofeminism 9

and more-than-human
  perspectives 42–3,
  46
ecological degradation 4
ecological games 139–40
Ecuador 49
educational institutions,
  animals as therapy
  in 12
Elephant Listening project
  82
Elias, Norbert 29, 30
emotional robotics see
  zoomorphic robots
Enlightenment, and animal
  ethics 33–4
environmental activism 9
environmental degradation
  4–5, 31
environmental protection
  125
environmental sustainability
  9, 10
  and animal activism 56
Equilinox 140
ethics
  animal ethics 26, 40,
    48–51, 160
    sentience 33–4, 36–7,
    46, 48, 161
  bioethics 34
  nomadic ethics 50, 161
  One Health approach to
    40
  wild ethics 50, 161
  and zoomorphic robots
    148–9

Index

Index

Index

Index

Index

Index

Index